A Practical Guide to Business Incubator Marketing

NBIA PUBLICATIONS

A Practical Guide to Business Incubator Marketing

By Corinne Colbert
NBIA Publications
Athens, Ohio

A Practical Guide to Business Incubator Marketing

Writer: Corinne Colbert
Editor: Meredith Erlewine
Designer: Claire Mullen
Printer: McNaughton & Gunn, Inc.

© 2007 NBIA Publications

National Business Incubation Association, Athens, Ohio

All Rights Reserved
Printed in the United States of America

This publication is a creative work copyrighted by the National Business Incubation Association and fully protected by all applicable copyright laws. Reproduction or translation of any part of this work beyond that permitted by Section 107 or 108 of the 1976 United States Copyright Act without the permission of the copyright owner is unlawful. Requests for permission or further information should be addressed to the Permission Department, NBIA Publications, 20 E. Circle Drive, #37198, Athens, Ohio 45701.

ISBN: 978-1-887183-65-9

This work has been made possible in part by support from @Wales Digital Media Initiative, the Louisiana Business & Technology Center at Louisiana State University and Louisiana Economic Development, the Northeast Indiana Innovation Center, and Strategic Development Services.

Contents

Acknowledgments v
Contributors vii
Introduction 1

Chapter 1: Conducting Market Research 3
    Market Research Basics 4
    Secondary Market Research 5
    Primary Market Research 8
    Using Market Research 14
    Identifying Potential Clients 15
    Identifying Potential Partners and Sponsors 18
    Positioning Your Program in the Local Market 19
    Fine-Tuning Your Services 23
    The Bottom Line 24

Chapter 1 Sidebars
    Resources for Learning More About Your Market 5
    Getting Help With Data Analysis 6
    Online Research Sources 7
    Survey Design Tips 9
    Making Market Knowledge Pay Off 10
    Ask Around for Opinions 13
    Getting Professional Marketing Help 15
    Give Your Audience What It Needs 16
    Targeting Promotions to Individual Markets 19
    Gauging Your Program's Reputation in the Industry 20
    Setting Prices for Space and Services 22
    Building and Maintaining a Marketing Database 25

Chapter 2: Creating a Marketing Plan 27
Elements of a Marketing Plan 28

Chapter 2 Sidebars
Getting Organized With a Marketing Plan 28
Twenty Questions: Developing Your Marketing Focus 30
Taking a SWOT at Your Program 31
Try Something Different 33
Defining Your Value Proposition 36

Chapter 3: Marketing Methods 39
Branding Your Incubator 39
Selecting Marketing Methods 42
Advertising 43
Direct Mail 48
Outreach 49
Public Relations 56
Publications 58
Networking 65

Chapter 3 Sidebars
What's in a Name? 40
Marketing Mistakes to Avoid 42
Harnessing the Power of Testimonials 44
Wearing a Logo on Your Sleeve 46
Playing by the Direct Mail Rules 48
Marketing Methods Overview 50
Keeping an Event Fresh and Relevant 53
Making the Most of a Trade Show Exhibit 55
Tips for Better Publicity Photos 57
Great Guides for Design and Writing 59
Tips for Optimum DIY Design 61
What to Put on Your Web Site 63
Reporting to the Community 65
Three Key Moments in Networking 67

Conclusion 69

Appendix A: Media Relations 71
    What Is News? 71
    Defining Your Target Audience 72
    Selecting Media Outlets 73
    Contacting the Media 73
    Distributing the News 74
    Radio and Television Promotions 77
    News Conferences 78
    Working With the Media 79
    Tips for Media Interviews 80
    How to Handle Bad News 80

    Appendix A Sidebars
    News Worth Reporting 72
    What to Put in a Press Kit 74
    Anatomy of a News Release 75
    News Release Add-Ons 76
    Holding a News Conference 79

Appendix B: Sources 83

Acknowledgments

A Practical Guide to Business Incubator Marketing was made possible in part by generous financial support from four NBIA members: @Wales Digital Media Initiative in Cardiff, Wales; the Louisiana Business & Technology Center at Louisiana State University in Baton Rouge, Louisiana, with support from Louisiana Economic Development; the Northeast Indiana Innovation Center in Fort Wayne, Indiana; and Strategic Development Services in Columbus, Ohio. The individuals affiliated with these member programs—Evan M. Jones, Charles F. D'Agostino, Karl R. LaPan, and Charles Stein, respectively—not only sponsored the book, but also were patient and thoughtful interview subjects. Each is a creative and successful marketer, and each understood the importance of disseminating information on incubator marketing. NBIA is grateful for their contributions of time and money to help bring this project to life.

This book got its start in 2004, when NBIA member Cameron Wold proposed that NBIA publish a book on incubator marketing plans. In the process of developing that idea, we determined that there was a need for a more holistic approach to the subject: one that would encompass not only marketing plans, but also market research and specific incubator marketing methods. We're grateful to Cameron for planting the seed that became this book—and for his help during the planning process.

This book also benefited from the insights and guidance of several more NBIA members, who served as a steering committee. NBIA thanks Charles F. D'Agostino, Julie Gustafson, Robert Hisrich, Even M. Jones, and Mark Lieberman, whose comments and suggestions helped us draft a working outline of the book. They also were among the first people interviewed for the book, and their answers helped to frame subsequent interviews.

When the manuscript was near completion, NBIA members again pitched in to help. Robert Hisrich and Lou Cooperhouse reviewed the final draft of the book, and their suggestions sharpened the text.

NBIA staff members also helped make this book a reality. Dinah Adkins offered advice and suggested resources, drawing on her decades of experience and extensive knowledge of individuals within the incubation industry. Mary Ann Gulino trolled the Internet to find the best of our members' Web sites, contacted dozens of members to ask them to send samples of their marketing collateral, and then kept track of who had sent what. She also was a huge help in fact-checking the finished manuscript.

What truly made the book, however, were the experiences and actual marketing samples shared by nearly fifty additional NBIA members and friends. They are the real stars of this project, and we are grateful to each of them for taking the time to talk with us and send us their brochures, newsletters, reports, and other materials. We hope you enjoy learning about them as much as we did.

Corinne Colbert
Meredith Erlewine

Contributors

Charles Allen, former director, Applied Process Engineering Laboratory, Richland, Washington

Tony Antoniades, general manager, Advanced Technology Development Center, Atlanta, Georgia

John L. Augustine III, senior director of economic and entrepreneurial development, Innovation Center @ Wilkes-Barre, Wilkes-Barre, Pennsylvania

Judith Barral, director, Fairfax Innovation Center, Fairfax, Virginia

Wayne Barz, manager of entrepreneurial services, Ben Franklin Technology Partners of Northeast Pennsylvania, Bethlehem, Pennsylvania

Hilla Barzilai-Abileah, director of marketing and communications, Houston Technology Center, Houston, Texas

Anne-Marie Birkill, CEO, i.lab Incubator, Toowong, Queensland, Australia

Patti Breedlove, manager, University of Florida Sid Martin Biotechnology Incubator, Alachua, Florida

David J. Cattey, former executive director, The Business Technology Center (now part of TechColumbus), Columbus, Ohio

Linda J. Clark, director, Ohio University Innovation Center, Athens, Ohio

Steven Clark, vice president, business incubation services, TechColumbus, Columbus, Ohio

Sandra Cochrane, chief operating officer, Southwest Michigan Innovation Center, Kalamazoo, Michigan

Lou Cooperhouse, director, Rutgers Food Innovation Center, New Brunswick, New Jersey

Charles F. D'Agostino, executive director, Louisiana Business & Technology Center, Louisiana State University, Baton Rouge, Louisiana

Jeanette DeDiemar, business marketing manager, @Wales Digital Media Initiative, Cardiff, Wales, and executive director, Integrated Marketing and Communications, University of Wisconsin Oshkosh

Jan DeYoung, executive director, St. Louis Enterprise Centers, St. Louis, Missouri

Glenn Doell, director, technology transfer, Greene, Tweed & Co., Kulpsville, Pennsylvania

Scott J. Drachnik, vice president of business development and marketing, Economic Development Center of St. Charles County, St. Peters, Missouri

Carol Ann Dykes, chief operating officer, University of Central Florida Technology Incubator, Orlando, Florida

Agnes Flemal, general manager, Wallonia Space Logistics, Liege, Belgium

Paul M. Frison, former president & CEO, Houston Technology Center, Houston, Texas

Contributors *(continued)*

Kelli Furtado, former chief operating officer, Central Valley Business Incubator, Clovis, California

Colin Graham, chief executive, Innovation Centre Sunshine Coast, Sippy Downs, Queensland, Australia

Jim Greenwood, president, Greenwood Consulting Group, Sanibel, Florida

Julie Gustafson, executive director, Amoskeag Business Incubator, Manchester, New Hampshire

Tim Haynes, vice president for member services and marketing, TechColumbus, Columbus, Ohio

Bonnie Herron, executive director, Gwinnett Innovation Park, Atlanta, Georgia

Vic Hess, senior vice president for small business development, Howard County Economic Development Agency, Columbia, Maryland

Robert Hisrich, Garvin Professor of Global Entrepreneurship and director, Thunderbird Global Incubator, Thunderbird School of Global Management, Glendale, Arizona

Ed Hobbs, general manager, Toronto Business Development Centre, Toronto, Ontario, Canada

Lisa Ison, president, The New Century Venture Center, Roanoke, Virginia

Vicki Jenings, director of business relations, Fitzsimons Redevelopment Authority, Aurora, Colorado

Evan M. Jones, head of digital and incubation, @Wales Digital Media Initiative, Cardiff, Wales

Deborah L. King, director, Springfield Business Incubator, Springfield Technical Community College, Springfield, Massachusetts

Karl R. LaPan, president & CEO, Northeast Indiana Innovation Center, Fort Wayne, Indiana

Carol Kraus Lauffer, partner, Business Cluster Development, Palo Alto, California

Mark Lieberman, manager of regional economic development, Business Technology Center of Los Angeles County, a project of the Community Development Commission of Los Angeles County, Altadena, California

David R. Lohr, executive director, Virginia Biosciences Development Center, Richmond, Virginia

Mark S. Long, president & CEO, Indiana University Emerging Technologies Center, Indianapolis, Indiana

Marie Longserre, president & CEO, Santa Fe Business Incubator, Santa Fe, New Mexico

Stephen Loy, director of communications, Louisiana Technology Park, Baton Rouge, Louisiana

Adele Lyons, former executive director, Gulf Coast Business Technology Center, Biloxi, Mississippi

Contributors *(continued)*

Stuart Miller, executive director, INC.*spire*, the Incubator Program of the Greater Reston Chamber of Commerce, Reston, Virginia

Aaron Miscenich, executive director, New Orleans BioInnovation Center, New Orleans, Louisiana

Suzanne Mitchell, director, Applied Process Engineering Laboratory, Richland, Washington

Tom O'Neal, CEO, University of Central Florida Technology Incubator, Orlando, Florida

Bonnie O'Regan, incubator manager, Florida/NASA Business Incubation Center, Titusville, Florida

Lisa S. Roberts, director, Business, Industry & Entrepreneurship Center, Cowley College, Arkansas City, Kansas

Lesley Anne Rubenstein, chief executive, Thames Innovation Centre, London, England

Donald C. Schutt, executive director, MidMichigan Innovation Center, Midland, Michigan

Dar Schwanbeck, managing director, Northern Alberta Business Incubator, St. Albert, Alberta, Canada

Jennifer Simon, CEO and president of the Economic Development Council, Athens Area Chamber of Commerce, Athens, Ohio

Lisa S. Smith, vice president of marketing and principal, ANGLE Technology, Charlottesville, Virginia

Charles Stein, president, Strategic Development Services, Columbus, Ohio

Tammi L. Thomas, director, marketing and business development, techcenter@UMBC Incubator and Accelerator, Baltimore, Maryland

Mildred Walters, executive director, Nashville Business Incubation Center, Nashville, Tennessee

Megan Watkins, former program and marketing associate, Women's Technology Cluster, San Francisco, California

Lynne Waymon, president, Contacts Count, Silver Spring, Maryland

Jasper Welch, director, San Juan College Enterprise Center, Farmington, New Mexico

Paul Wetenhall, president, High Tech Rochester's Lennox Tech Enterprise Center, Rochester, New York

Jon M. Wilder, executive director, Ceramics Corridor Innovation Centers, Alfred and Corning/Painted Post, New York

Peter Wohl, executive director, Adirondack Regional Business Incubator, Glens Falls, New York

Mary Zilar, facility property management coordinator, Applied Process Engineering Laboratory, Richland, Washington

Introduction

As an incubator manager, you're a busy person. You advise clients, inform stakeholders, manage staff, and maintain your facility, among other duties. Chances are, you know that marketing is important, too, but it might be far down on your list of priorities.

If that's the case, you may want to reshuffle your priorities. Your incubation program is a business like any other and, as you probably tell your clients, marketing is one of the pillars of business success.

Marketing can help keep your incubator full, and maintaining a full incubator is the linchpin of a sustainable program. "Success depends on keeping a steady flow of viable clients into the incubator," says Charles F. D'Agostino, executive director of the Louisiana Business & Technology Center, the incubation program at Louisiana State University in Baton Rouge, Louisiana.

Even when your incubator is full and you have a waiting list, though, you still need to market the program. Marketing isn't just about clients. It's about distinguishing your incubation program from your competition, whether that competition comes from other incubators or from other economic development initiatives or commercial landlords. (Bear in mind that you're competing not only for clients, but also for funding and other forms of support.) Marketing is how you establish and maintain your program's reputation within the community. Through marketing, you attract not only new clients, but also partners and sponsors that can support and sustain your incubation program.

Good marketing doesn't have to be expensive. Some of the most effective marketing methods are low- or no-cost options: networking, cultivating relationships, and using the Web and e-mail. Remember: anything you do that puts your incubator, its achievements, and its capabilities in front of an audience that can affect your program—potential and current clients, stakeholders, the public—is marketing.

Of course, some marketing tasks do require money. Throughout this book, you'll meet incubator managers who have leveraged their relationships with partners and sponsors to cover part or all of the cost of big-ticket items such as design, printing, advertising, or catering for large events.

You don't necessarily need a big staff to market effectively, either. Members of your board of directors, partners and supporters, and students from a nearby college or university all can help you spread your message. "We've made it a part of our policy that we hire interns [from nearby Southern New Hampshire University] on a regular basis" for marketing, says Julie Gustafson, executive director of the Amoskeag Business Incubator in Manchester, New Hampshire. She's built relationships with the university's career development department, as well as individual professors. "I have two interns now just because teachers said, 'I have someone good for you,'" Gustafson says.

She also calls upon her board of directors, especially during events held at the incubator. "I try to get the whole board to attend events because I can only do so much," she says.

What marketing will cost you, however, is time. The incubator managers interviewed for this book estimated that they spent between 15 percent and 30 percent of their time in a given week on marketing activities. That may seem like a lot, especially when you're overextended as it is. But you're probably already doing many of the same things these managers are doing: writing and mailing press releases, speaking at Rotary lunches, and meeting with stakeholders.

While that's a good start, truly effective marketing requires thought and planning. "Shotgun marketing is a mistake I see a lot, where there's no proper identification of [who] the audience is," says Evan M. Jones, head of digital and incubation with the @Wales Digital Media Initiative in Cardiff, Wales. "It's nice to see your ad in papers or hear about your incubator on the radio, but [you have] to say, 'How many potential entrepreneurs are going to hear this? How many are in [our niche]? How many are going to read our ad or listen to it while turning right at a busy junction?'"

That's where this book comes in. We've talked with incubator managers who already make savvy use of marketing techniques to promote their programs. You don't have to do everything you'll read about here. The idea is for you to see what your options are and put them together in a comprehensive marketing strategy that works for your incubator.

How This Book Can Help

In chapter 1, you'll learn how to use market research to identify potential clients, partners, and sponsors; learn more about your current clients and graduates; and match your offerings to their needs. **Chapter 2** tells you how to create a marketing plan, the backbone of your marketing efforts. **Chapter 3** is an overview of the marketing methods you're most likely to find effective in terms of cost and return on investment, with real-world examples from incubation professionals. **At the back of the book** you'll find a special section devoted specifically to media relations, as well as a CD-ROM filled with examples of marketing materials from incubation programs around the world.

CHAPTER 1
Conducting Market Research

When NBIA first started asking members about how they conduct market research, it seemed as if there were two kinds of incubation professionals: those who find market research indispensable and do it often, and those who for lack of time and resources don't do it at all.

By digging a little deeper, though, we learned that almost every incubator does some type of market research—it just doesn't always take the form of an in-depth, formal study. "There is a broad spectrum of [ways] you can handle research," says Carol Kraus Lauffer, partner in Business Cluster Development, an incubation consulting firm in Palo Alto, California. "It doesn't have to be an onerous task; you can make it simple."

For many incubators, market research can be as simple as asking community leaders a few questions. "Even when you run into people at events, ask them who they work with and what their challenges are," Lauffer says. "If you're out there in the community talking about the incubator, you should be getting feedback on the market as well."

Incubators that do extensive or formal research tend to be those associated with universities or corporations—in other words, incubators whose stakeholders want or expect hard data to prove a return on their investment. "We have to show measurements," says Tammi L. Thomas, director of marketing and business development for techcenter@UMBC, the technology incubator of the University of Maryland, Baltimore County in Baltimore, Maryland. "We can't just say anecdotally, 'We think'—we have to put it on paper and have numbers."

Longtime managers often are comfortable with a more informal approach to market research. "If I were just starting out or hadn't had a lot of business experience, if I hadn't done a lot of marketing at the company level, I might want that comfort of having gone through all the right processes," says Bonnie Herron, executive director of the Gwinnett Innovation Park in Atlanta, Georgia. She's been in incubation for nearly twenty years and has served as a senior officer with several technology corporations. "[Your need for formal research] has to do with your comfort level with what you've done in the past, your budget, and [stakeholders'] expectations." Herron gets feedback from her clients and stakeholders the old-fashioned way: she just asks them for their opinions.

Whether your research is formal or informal, it's vital. In most cases, an incubator does market research from the outset—specifically, research performed for the incubator's feasibility study. But that research is most likely focused on whether the market can support an incubator, not how to communicate to that market.

"You do market research most heavily when you're developing the incubator because you need to make sure you have some real information on where to locate, what kind of services to offer, what facilities will be in most demand, and what size offices you need," says Robert Hisrich, Garvin Professor of Global Entrepreneurship and director of the Thunderbird Global Incubator at the Thunderbird School of Global Management in Glendale, Arizona.

A good feasibility study will have some basic information you can use for marketing, particularly identification of stakeholders and characteristics of the entrepreneurial pool (e.g., the types of businesses being started and the services they might need). But you will need more information than that to market your incubation program effectively in the long run. "The market is constantly changing," says Charles Stein, president of Strategic Development Services, a consulting firm in Columbus, Ohio, that specializes in incubator development and funding. "When you do a feasibility study for an incubator, it's at a particular point in time. After that time, things start to change; there are always new players moving into the market. You've got to constantly stay on top of the market."

Unfortunately, too many incubators dive right into promotional activities without conducting research beyond their feasibility study, says Lisa S. Smith, vice president of marketing and a principal with ANGLE Technology, an international consulting firm in Charlottesville, Virginia, that plans and operates incubators. "Everybody wants dessert first," she says. "You have to look at the market first."

Market research is more than just collecting data. "You're not only digging up the information, but also analyzing it," Smith says. "You have to analyze the market to understand what's happening." For example, she says, acquiring a list of applicants for business licenses not only gives you contact information for potential clients, but also a glimpse at business trends. "The kinds of companies getting started in a community indicates where new business interest is," she says. Look carefully at what you find for broader or future implications for your program.

You can accomplish myriad tasks through market research: characterizing potential clients, identifying possible partners and sponsors, aligning your services with clients' needs, and so on. Before we get into those details, though, let's look at how market research works.

Market Research Basics

There are two main types of market research: primary research, in which you get data directly from individuals or groups through surveys or interviews, and secondary research, which draws on collections of data that already have been assembled by others.

While secondary resources can provide general information about the environment in which your program operates, primary research probably will prove more useful

Resources for Learning More About Your Market

Government
- U.S. Census Bureau economic data
- State records of incorporation
- State employment commission
- Municipal or county offices that issue building permits, occupancy permits, and business licenses
- Regional Small Business Administration office
- Manufacturing Extension Partnership
- Small Business Development Centers (SBDCs)
- SBA-backed and other microloan programs

Trade and professional associations
- Industry councils
- Inventors clubs
- SCORE, Counselors to America's Small Business

Professionals
- Attorneys, accountants, and other professionals
- Local chapters of professional development organizations and associations
- Venture capital firms
- Angel investment organizations
- Seed capital funds

Business and economic development organizations
- Economic development agencies
- Chambers of commerce
- Entrepreneur training programs
- Economic development departments of utility companies
- Targeted business assistance programs (women, minorities, veterans, etc.)

Other
- Existing companies undergoing or likely to undergo downsizing
- Incubators in your region
- University faculty and researchers
- University offices of research and/or technology commercialization
- University and college continuing education programs (including noncredit courses)
- University and college centers for economic development

---

in learning about your market. "It's fine to look at demographics and competition," says Jim Greenwood, president of Greenwood Consulting Group in Sanibel, Florida, and a former incubator manager. "In my opinion, unless you survey potential clients, you are running a big risk of convincing yourself that a market exists based on secondary data like community demographics when, for whatever reason, the reality is that no one locally [would actually use incubator services]."

Secondary resources may show general business trends, but may not disclose much information about start-ups, which may not leave a public paper trail, such as property tax returns or business license applications. "Start-ups are under the radar screen," Lauffer says. "It's not [as if] you can get a list of start-ups and survey them."

That's not to say that secondary research isn't worthwhile. Collected and published information available from a variety of sources can help you assemble a mailing list, choose appropriate media outlets for advertising and publicity, and learn about trends in business incubation and economic development.

Secondary Market Research

Despite its name, secondary research is most often the first step in a research project because it provides broad, easily accessible data about your market. Here are some sources of secondary information.

Government agencies. Local, state, and federal governments keep meticulous records that can be helpful in your research. The U.S. Small Business Administration keeps economic profiles of every state; the

U.S. Department of Agriculture's Economic Research Service provides demographic and economic data down to the state and county levels. State departments of commerce, labor, or economic development also are gold mines of business data.

State and federal data often are available online, but county and metropolitan information may not be; the more rural the area, the more likely you'll need to do your research in person, rather than online. For example, the Economic Development Center of St. Charles County in St. Peters, Missouri, got a list of the holders of and applicants for business licenses from the city government. "We pulled together a [mailing] list from that database," says Scott J. Drachnik, the EDC's vice president of business development and marketing.

Another good source of local data is the nearest Small Business Development Center. The U.S. Small Business Administration requires SBDCs to keep records on the businesses it serves. SBDCs also have access to SBDCNet, a database of information kept by SBDCs nationwide. "You can get results quicker than the typical person would take to look for data," says Lisa S. Roberts, a former market research consultant who is now director of the Business, Industry & Entrepreneurship Center at Cowley College in Arkansas City, Kansas.

The Internet. Search engines such as Google or Yahoo! can help you identify resources you might not be aware of otherwise, while an online encyclopedia such as Wikipedia can provide background information to inform your work. (A note of caution, however: always be sure to check the source of any information published online. Because the Web is so easily accessible, almost anyone can publish pretty much anything, accurate or not.) Vast quantities of government data also are available online, including U.S. Census Bureau analyses and industry studies from the U.S. Department of Labor's Bureau of Labor Statistics. (See "Online Research Sources" on page 7.)

Libraries. Sure, many of the resources available at the library also are available online. But the library has something the Internet doesn't: real live librarians. "You can get a librarian to introduce you to lots of resources in a short time that you eventually may have stumbled on [online]," Smith says. "And as you continue with your research, you'll have someone you can call on whose business it is to know those resources." In addition, Smith says, many libraries are creating small-business sections in their facilities that bring together printed and online materials in a single space.

Getting Help With Data Analysis

To the uninitiated, the reams of data available from government and business sources can seem like so much gibberish. What exactly do all those numbers mean? Is any of what you're seeing really useful?

"Data is data," says Lisa S. Roberts, a former market research consultant who is now director of the Business, Industry & Entrepreneurship Center at Cowley College in Arkansas City, Kansas. "It's not useful until it becomes information. It's understanding it not only from the research side, but also the implications."

You don't have to be an expert in data analysis—not when there probably are experts around who would be willing to help. "There are people out there who know how to turn data into information," Roberts says. So if a commercial real-estate firm, financial institution, or local media outlet has agreed to share its market statistics with you, "Ask them, 'Is there someone in your office who works with this data who feels confident explaining it to me and how it applies to my business decisions?'" Roberts says.

Business and economic development organizations. One of the best places to get information about your local business community is the chamber of commerce. "My first stop in secondary data is always the chamber of commerce," Hisrich says. "They have enormous amounts of data, and they're happy to share because you're going to affect the area's economy." Many chambers of commerce will have business and population demographics, links to economic and business development agencies and organizations, lists of civic organizations, and information about development incentive programs. At the very least, the chamber will have a directory of area businesses with addresses and phone numbers, which can help you locate banks, attorneys, CPAs, and other professionals who come in contact with entrepreneurs.

Don't overlook your local college or university; public institutions, in particular, have community development missions and thus are likely to be happy to help you. "Universities increasingly have offices of economic development," Smith says. "Some universities even have economic development consulting operations, and those are good people to know."

Businesses. Commercial realtors, utility companies, financial institutions, and media outlets all keep or have access to market research data, Roberts says. For example, a commercial realtor may be able to give you detailed data on the population's incomes and spending habits—information that could help you pinpoint places to look for sponsors or donors to a capital campaign.

Newspapers and TV and radio stations have to know who their readers and listeners are to woo advertisers. Say you know that your clients tend to be men in their mid-thirties whose average income is $45,000. Chances are, a media outlet will know exactly which newspaper they read, TV stations they watch, and radio stations they tune into.

Any of these resources is likely to be willing to share its data with you, Roberts says. "Commercial lenders have always been a great resource for me because they want to see new businesses start and be successful," she says. Of course, their motives (and those of realtors and media outlets) aren't purely altruistic; they should see you as a potential supplier of clients for them down the road.

Trade and professional associations. These days, it seems that there's a professional

Online Research Sources

Charles Stein, president of Strategic Development Services—a consulting firm in Columbus, Ohio, that specializes in incubator development and funding—recommends these Web sites as places to start when conducting market research:

- **American Fact Finder.** Among other quick-search functions, this U.S. Census Bureau site lets you plug in a ZIP code to get a full demographic profile of your community, including maps. *www.factfinder.census.gov*
- **Economic Census.** Every five years, the U.S. Census Bureau collects a vast range of data on businesses, which is then broken down from the national to the local level. The Web site also allows users to search its results by North American Industry Classification System (NAICS) code to find data on specific industries. *www.census.gov/econ/census02/*
- **Your state's department of commerce, labor, or economic development.** "Most state economic development Web sites have sections that are helpful," Stein says. He cites the example of Maryland's Department of Business and Economic Development (*www.choosemaryland.org*), which offers detailed information on industry sectors, population, transportation, and other factors that affect economic development.

association for nearly every imaginable industry. Some of these organizations, such as state technology councils or agricultural commodity associations, can be valuable for identifying and reaching niche markets. Others—incubation associations and venture capital and angel groups—offer the prospect of networking and possible partnerships.

In some cases, an association can serve both purposes. Julie Gustafson, executive director of the Amoskeag Business Incubator in Manchester, New Hampshire, reaches software developers and service providers tied to the state's software and Internet industries through a partnership with the Software Association of New Hampshire. The association holds events at her incubator free of charge; in return, it promotes the incubator via its listserv and has given Gustafson a free booth at its yearly exposition. "I know this relationship has helped us broaden public awareness and in promoting the incubator to software companies," Gustafson says.

Your own industry association, NBIA, can provide you with information about trends, characteristics, and practices. "A lot [of our research] has been through NBIA," Gustafson says. In addition to providing data on the overall business incubation industry, NBIA can connect you with other incubators in your state and region so you can compare your program and services to theirs.

Primary Market Research

In primary market research, you collect information personally through surveys (mailed, e-mailed, online, or telephone) or interviews with individuals or groups. This will flesh out the more general data you collect using secondary sources.

For the first six years of his incubator's existence, Jasper Welch, director of the San Juan College Enterprise Center in Farmington, New Mexico, gathered feedback on his program and services with short questionnaires and informal discussions. By spring 2006, though, he was ready for a more formal approach. "We felt we had enough history that we could ask our customers how we were doing." He hired a professional researcher for two interview studies: one of stakeholders and another with clients and graduates.

"Before, we were kind of guessing along the way and talking to our customers [informally]," he says. "But in terms of larger programmatic adjustments, you probably need to go out and [survey] people."

Primary research involves at least three steps: setting a research goal, which determines what questions you will ask; choosing a population sample, which determines who will answer your questions; and selecting a research method, which determines how you will ask your questions.

Setting a research goal. To get good research results, start with a clear idea of what you want to learn and how you will use that information. That will determine the kinds of questions you will need to ask. Objectives of primary research may include:

- Gathering information from current clients to determine the best marketing method to reach potential clients
- Learning what potential clients need, want, or expect from the incubator to determine facility or service offerings
- Learning current clients' and/or graduates' opinions of the incubator to improve or expand services
- Collecting community opinions about the incubator to gauge support for a capital campaign or other incubator need

Notice that each of these goals has a specific objective tied to it. You're not just going to collect information about your clients because you want to know them better; you want to use that information for a particular purpose (say, to choose the most effective marketing method to reach new clients). Primary research requires an investment of time and varying amounts of money; you don't want to waste that investment.

The Rutgers Food Innovation Center launched in 2001 as an incubator without walls. After four years without a physical facility, it had already assisted more than five hundred clients all over the state—a track record that was a big help as Director Lou Cooperhouse raised the $7.4 million he needed to build and equip a 23,000-square-foot building. To learn what potential clients might need in the facility, he conducted focus groups with the heads of small food-based businesses throughout New Jersey.

"I [wanted] to know what equipment would be truly innovative, what services our clients [couldn't] get from the private sector or would trust more if they came from our center," Cooperhouse says. "And how [could] we aggregate some of our offerings, such as product development, analytical testing, and consumer research?"

With a goal in mind, you can start thinking about the questions you should ask to get the information you need. For example, if you want to learn what potential clients need or want from an incubator, you might ask questions like these:

- What does the company sell, service, or manufacture? The types of businesses that exist or are starting in your area can affect both your facility and your services. If there are a lot of catering and specialty food companies, for example, you might want to add a shared kitchen.

Survey Design Tips

You're more likely to get willing participants for a survey, and get more accurate results, if your questionnaire is well-designed. The survey should look easy to complete, and the instructions should be clear and consistent throughout.

Here are some guidelines from Creative Research Systems of Petaluma, California, which creates market-research software and provides other services for researchers.

- **Keep it neat and simple.** The more ink there is on the page, the more work the survey will seem to be, so use as much white space as possible. Don't use lines to separate survey sections, and eliminate extra punctuation marks, such as a period after a question number.
- **Think circles, not squares.** Set up the survey so respondents circle their answers. That keeps the visual overload of lines or boxes to a minimum and also makes their choices very clear to them (less chance of marking the wrong box) and to you (less chance of data input error).
- **Go long, not wide.** Response categories that go horizontally across the page require check-off lines or boxes. That makes the page look crowded and can be confusing for respondents to know what line or box goes with what answer. Line up answer choices vertically under the question.
- **Lure them in.** Put the easiest questions up front; save the tough ones for later, after respondents have built up some momentum. End with easy choices again, such as the respondent's name, address, telephone number, e-mail address, and Web address.
- **Keep like with like.** Group questions that use the same response categories (e.g., excellent, good, fair, poor) or are related in subject matter (e.g., demographics, services, infrastructure needs).

- What is the company's potential for growth? You'll want to know if the company fits with your facility (will it grow too fast for the space available?) and your program. "If they're early-stage companies and I know they're going to need … money, I might ask, 'Will they be able to pay the monthly fees?'" Smith says. "Maybe I'm going to target companies that already have cash flow."
- How long has the company been in business? Less experienced entrepreneurs will need more help with business basics, while more experienced ones will appreciate advanced services such as access to capital or help with intellectual property rights.
- What type of facilities does the company need? If you're developing an incubator, you don't want to find out after building office space that manufacturing bays are in high demand among local entrepreneurs. Biotech companies will need wet labs. A manufacturing company will need loading docks. Companies with far-flung clients may want videoconferencing for virtual meetings. If your market includes such companies, you might want to add—and tout—the amenities they're seeking.
- What kinds of business assistance services does the company need or want? Offer a list of suggestions, such as business planning, business counseling, mentoring, networking activities, marketing help, links to community resources, and access to capital. (NBIA's *State of the Business Incubation Industry* reports include a list of services offered by incubation programs.) You may want to have respondents rank their choices.
- What services would the company pay

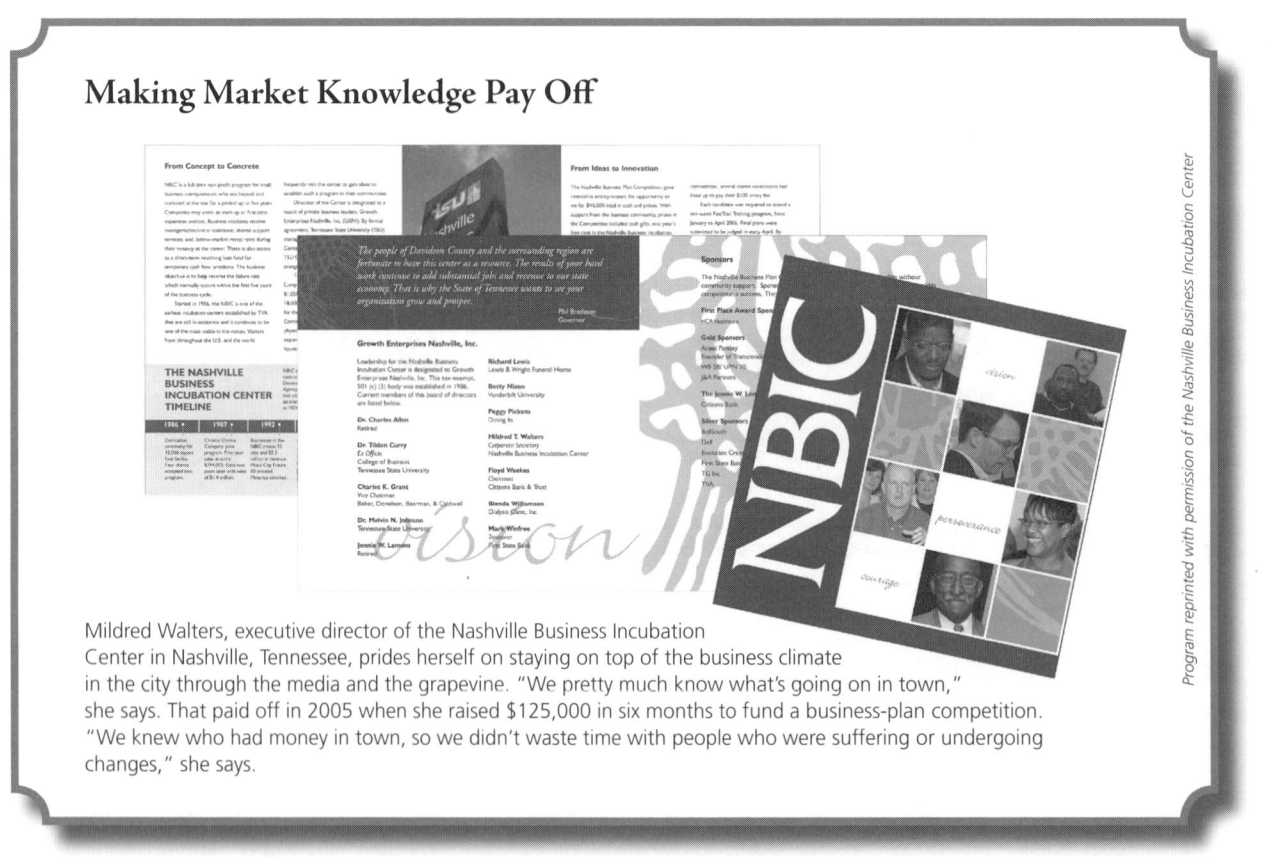

Making Market Knowledge Pay Off

Mildred Walters, executive director of the Nashville Business Incubation Center in Nashville, Tennessee, prides herself on staying on top of the business climate in the city through the media and the grapevine. "We pretty much know what's going on in town," she says. That paid off in 2005 when she raised $125,000 in six months to fund a business-plan competition. "We knew who had money in town, so we didn't waste time with people who were suffering or undergoing changes," she says.

Program reprinted with permission of the Nashville Business Incubation Center

10 A Practical Guide to Business Incubator Marketing

for? How much? Questions like these can help you set a price for your services by showing what value clients place on them.

Sometimes, your list of questions may arise from questions you've already asked. At UMBC, Thomas surveyed clients about incubator services not only to collect feedback, but also to prepare for focus groups with entrepreneurs who might be interested in entering the incubator. "[The survey] led us to being able to ask the right questions [in the focus groups] and have the right people at the table," she says.

Regardless of the specific questions you ask, you will want them to be concise, easily understood, and worded neutrally to avoid bias. Ask for only one thing at a time; in the example above, for instance, you would ask one question about which services potential clients would pay for and another question about how much they would pay for them. Include options such as "not applicable," "don't know," "none," or "other"; while such responses won't tell you much, they'll keep respondents' frustration at a minimum if they don't have an answer to a question. (If you use "other," be sure to include a space for the respondent to write in an answer.)

"You don't want questions to be too complicated or too long," Smith says. She prefers using mostly multiple-choice questions and ending with a few open-ended questions, such as asking for recommendations or referrals. "We always get good input from that," Smith says.

Don't be afraid to be blunt, says Mark S. Long, president & CEO of the Indiana University Emerging Technologies Center in Indianapolis, Indiana. "Ask the questions you want to ask," he says. On a survey conducted during the incubator's development, Long asked respondents point-blank if they would be willing to give money to help build the IUETC facility. "I got a lot of noes," he says. "But I got several yesses."

The surprises, though, may not always be pleasant. "The day you get results back is not an easy day in the life of an incubator manager," Welch says. "There are always things they don't think you're doing a good job in."

What you do with the information you collect will depend in part on your incubator's stage of development. Asking questions about the types of space clients want can help a new or developing incubator configure offices and make decisions about including wet labs or high-bay manufacturing spaces. A more established incubator can use answers to those same questions to justify an expansion or capital campaign for a new facility, or tweak its communications to rectify misperceptions about the incubator's goals and activities.

Many incubators use economic impact data to show their stakeholders that their investments in incubation are paying off. For example, techcenter@UMBC used a professional market research firm to conduct an economic impact study. The study generated a wide array of measurements of the incubator's effect on the economy, so Thomas can tailor her messages to various stakeholders. "The university, state, and county have invested so much in the incubator and the research park," she says. "We'll be able to say to the county that for every dollar they invested in us, they get $7 back. For the university, we can say that one hundred jobs have been created for UMBC grads and one thousand students have been touched by companies that have come through here."

Choosing a population sample. Once you know what you're going to ask, the next step is to decide who, exactly, is going to answer those questions. Unless you're seeking information about a relatively small group (such as your current clients), you can't survey or interview everyone in a given market. What you need is a sample, or a group of people that represents your target market.

One factor in choosing a sample is the sample size. The more people who answer your questions, the more accurate the results will be—but it's also more work to collect, collate, and analyze the data. There isn't a linear relationship between sample size and accuracy, though; you won't get results that are twice as accurate from a sample size that's twice as big. Look at how much time and money you have to devote to the research project and sample accordingly.

"You want to be practical and realistic about the sample you're going to work with," Smith says. "Most incubators don't do large-scale samples because they don't have the luxury" of devoting chunks of staff time to creating, contacting, recording, and analyzing responses from lots of people.

The other primary factor in sampling is the type of sample you use. Random sampling ensures that each member of the larger target market has an equal chance of being included in the interview or survey. Statistically speaking, the more random the sample, the more accurate the results will be.

But random sampling is not as simple as choosing, say, every third contact on a mailing list. The sample group should have the proportions of certain populations—in terms of gender, age, company type, stage of development, and so on—as the target market. You may need help in generating a random sample for a large research project; this is a good time to seek advice from a professional marketing firm or a marketing professor at your local university. (See "Getting Professional Marketing Help" on page 15.)

"You probably want a representative sample, as opposed to a statistically significant sample, because of the sheer numbers of people you would have to get to be statistically relevant," Smith says.

When he was developing his incubator, Long turned to the NBIA member directory to look for programs similar to his in size, location, and mission. He called sixteen and visited another eleven in person, always with the same question. "I asked, 'What did you do right?'" Long says.

Selecting a research method. Primary research falls into two broad categories: surveys and interviews. Surveys are best for collecting fairly straightforward data, such as general demographics or rankings of particular needs, that don't need further explanation by the respondent. Surveys also are preferred for larger research projects because they can be distributed to a wider group of potential respondents.

In 2006, Thomas oversaw three surveys of more than forty incubator clients and research-park residents on behalf of techcenter@UMBC: one about the incubator's Web site, another on the incubator's services, and a third about networking events. "In each one of those surveys, we asked [respondents] questions about their demographics so we would know where we could go to recruit more companies like the ones we have," she says.

Interviews are better for measuring less tangible matters, such as opinions and feelings, because they're conducted in person; the interviewer can see body language and hear nuances of speech. That personal touch, though, can be expensive, and limits the number of people who can participate.

Cooperhouse spent about $10,000 on a series of focus groups held over four months. The cost included the services of an experienced focus-group facilitator, who designed a discussion guide to help the focus groups run smoothly and efficiently; the cost of renting a facility with one-way mirrors and audiovisual recording; stipends paid to participants; and refreshments served during the sessions. But he feels the money was well spent, both in terms of the information he collected and

Ask Around for Opinions

Brochure reprinted with permission of Gwinnett Innovation Park

Nothing beats going to the source when making marketing decisions. When the Intelligent Systems Incubator in Atlanta, Georgia, changed its name to the Gwinnett Innovation Park in 2005, Executive Director Bonnie Herron ran the program's new name and graphic identity past current clients and some other local companies for their opinions. "We asked, 'Would you feel good about being associated with this name?'" she says. "Everybody was very positive about it."

---

the contacts he made with CEOs of food and beverage companies in New Jersey, who were the targets of the focus groups. "The process helped us identify people who have an interest in seeing how this facility might be of assistance to their business," he says.

Following is a list of various research methods with their pros and cons, as described by Creative Research Services, a research consulting firm based in Petaluma, California.

- **E-mail surveys** may be the least expensive option; there is no cost for postage or printing. And because users can respond instantly, you can generate data quickly. On the down side, your sample is limited to those who use e-mail. There's also the risk that your e-mail will get caught in recipients' spam filters (or that the recipients themselves will trash the message as spam).
- **Web surveys** also are inexpensive, although you can spring for an online survey service to prevent multiple responses and other survey errors. Like e-mail, Web surveys generate data quickly; but also like e-mail, a Web survey is limited to a particular population (those who have Internet access or are comfortable on the Web). Users may quit in mid-survey, leaving you with lopsided results. An online survey service can help you jump technical hurdles; most are user-friendly and aimed at amateur researchers. On the other hand, hosting the survey on your own Web site is free or at least low cost—and it will drive traffic to your site.
- **Mailed surveys** have the widest reach since almost everyone receives mail. But a piece of paper can be easily lost, and users have to take the extra step of dropping the survey into a mailbox

(instead of just clicking as they would in an e-mail or Web survey). And even if the user responds quickly, weeks may elapse between the time you mail the survey and the time you collect enough responses to generate useful data. Direct mail companies generally are happy with a response rate of 1 percent to 5 percent, so you have to throw a wide net.

The choice of an electronic survey versus a paper one may come down to your audience. UMBC's Thomas swears by SurveyMonkey, a Web survey service. She used the service initially because its basic features are free, but she has since upgraded to the professional version to gain more features. When given a choice between a paper survey and a Web option, "most of our responses were done online," Thomas says. But since her target market is technology companies, her audience is more familiar with a high-tech approach. Rutgers' Cooperhouse, who works with farmers and agriculture-based businesses, prefers paper because it seems more permanent and substantial—and thus important—to those surveyed. Plus, he says, "We are able to customize and personalize the form with a cover letter and use a postage-paid return envelope to increase our return rate."

- **Phone surveys** are almost a hybrid of surveys and interviews, since a caller will have direct contact with respondents. Phone surveys can yield data quickly. Disadvantages include the likelihood of hang-ups, screened calls, busy signals, or unanswered phones. You also will have to pay for the services of a phone bank.

If your audience is small, however, you can do phone surveys inexpensively, especially if you have access to interns from a nearby college or university. During his incubator's start-up phase, Long had a student intern comb through the NBIA member directory to find incubators similar to IUETC—university-based technology programs in the Midwest—and call them to see if they would share information about pricing and services. "And by golly, about 70 percent of them did," Long says. Using that information, Long set prices for incubator space, programs, and services such as copying.

- **Personal interviews,** whether individual or focus groups, allow for more complex questions and follow-up discussion, so you can get depth that surveys can't match. You'll pay for it though. You'll get the best results from hiring a professional interviewer who can guide the discussion, and that may not be cheap. You'll also have to pay for space for the interviews, the interviewer's travel, and incentives for participants.

Some of the best personal interviews, though, are as informal as can be. Whenever Long speaks to a community or professional organization, he makes sure he has time to chat with those in attendance. "You can do a ton of networking and ask, 'What's your real opinion?'" he says. It's not an idle question, either: "I take a pad and pencil and I write it all down," he says.

Using Market Research

So now you know why you should conduct market research and how you can go about it. The only thing left is to look at ways to use market research to help you meet your incubation program goals:

- Identifying potential clients
- Identifying potential partners and sponsors
- Positioning your program in the local market

- Fine-tuning your lineup of services

These activities are the foundation of an effective marketing effort.

Identifying Potential Clients

Think about all the small businesses within the area your incubator serves. There may be home-based businesses that are ready to leave the nest or spin-off companies of a large corporation. A nearby university may be producing research that could lead to medical or technological products. Perhaps your community has a large minority population; a military base may mean you have lots of

Getting Professional Marketing Help

While many marketing tasks can be handled in-house, it sometimes pays to hire a pro. This need not break the budget; in fact, you probably can get the work done at a significant discount or even for free, says Charles Stein, president of Strategic Development Services, a consulting firm in Columbus, Ohio, that specializes in incubator development and funding.

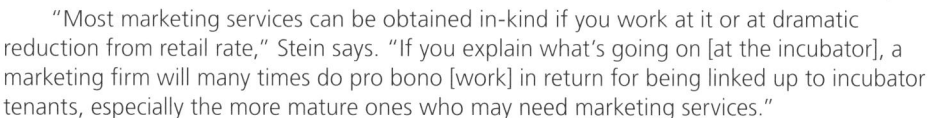

"Most marketing services can be obtained in-kind if you work at it or at dramatic reduction from retail rate," Stein says. "If you explain what's going on [at the incubator], a marketing firm will many times do pro bono [work] in return for being linked up to incubator tenants, especially the more mature ones who may need marketing services."

For example, the Indiana University Emerging Technologies Center in Indianapolis, Indiana, got a reduced price for the services of a public relations firm that developed the incubator's logo, marketing materials, and Web site before the incubator opened in 2003. The total cost was about $3,000—$2,000 less than the retail rate, says President & CEO Mark S. Long. "They knew we didn't have a lot of money and they wanted us as a client," he says.

One way to get professional help at a lower cost is to work with a university. Donald C. Schutt, executive director of the MidMichigan Innovation Center in Midland, Michigan, turned to a local university for help with a 2006 research project. Faculty from the university checked Schutt's questionnaire for bias that could influence responses, and also linked him with a graduate student who conducted the actual interviews.

Professional help may be the best choice if your project is complex or time-consuming. The University of Florida Sid Martin Biotechnology Incubator in Alachua, Florida, hired a market research firm to conduct a national survey of peer institutions, as well as interviews with incubator clients, in 2000. The job took the pros six months—time that a small incubation staff probably doesn't have.

Another reason to hire a pro is to keep an arm's-length distance from the project. "People may not tell us what we found out [had they not been] talking to a third party," says Jasper Welch, director of the San Juan College Enterprise Center in Farmington, New Mexico. Welch hired a professional researcher to interview stakeholders, clients, and graduates.

Incubator professionals who have worked with marketing and public relations firms say that the results were better than they could have achieved on their own. "I needed a map to guide us through marketing and to get better deal flow through the incubator," says Stephen Loy, director of communications for the Louisiana Technology Park in Baton Rouge, Louisiana. "I have a public relations and media background, not a marketing background."

And the payoff can be big. The same public relations firm that created IUETC's logo also arranged a grand opening gala, which drew nearly four hundred people to the incubator. "We raised over a half-million dollars" as a result of the event, Long says. One of the guests had sold the incubator a generator. He was so impressed by what he saw at the gala, Long says, "He asked me how much we paid for [the generator] and he wrote me a check [for that amount] on the spot."

veterans in the region. Each of these groups is a market segment, or a target market—businesses that could become your clients.

"You want to learn enough about your [potential] clients that you can devise a strategy to reach them," says ANGLE's Smith. "You want to see if they're start-ups, early-stage companies, folks who are already clients of programs such as SBDCs and are looking for a place to land, or people who are working in the garage."

Before you engage in the segmentation process, take a look at your incubator's feasibility study, which may include market segmentation. For a newer incubator or one in a rural area, that may be all that's needed. But a more established incubator that wants to refresh its program, or an incubator in an urban area with competition for clients, may find it helpful to re-segment its market.

Consumer markets often are segmented by demographics (age, occupation, family size, etc.), geography, behavior (e.g., knowledge or usage of a product or service), and psychographic factors (e.g., lifestyle, values). A business incubator's market for clients, on the other hand, may be segmented by geography, industry type, size, or stage of business, among other categories.

For example, when the NeoTech Incubator in Columbia, Maryland, wanted to expand its services to remain competitive among the state's twenty-plus incubators, it hired Strategic Development Services' Stein

Give Your Audience What It Needs

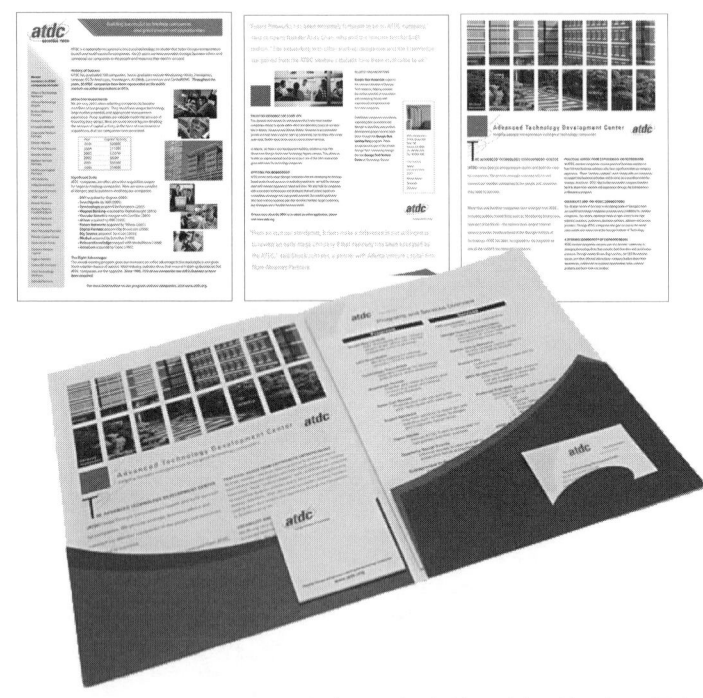

Different markets require different marketing messages. A cost-effective way to deliver information comes from the Advanced Technology Development Center in Atlanta, Georgia, which customizes a packet of materials for prospective clients and partners in pre-printed folders. General Manager Tony Antoniades ordered 1,000 folders printed in ATDC's colors on a heavy, smooth, matte stock. He fills the folder with information targeted to the recipient. For example, potential investors receive a list of ATDC clients and a single-page investor sheet that lists current data on investments and investors in ATDC clients, as well as mergers and acquisitions. He has a similar one-sheet brochure for ATDC itself that explains what the program is and what it does, which he includes for potential clients.

Brochures reprinted with permission of the Advanced Technology Development Center; folder photo by Suzanne Burkey

A Practical Guide to Business Incubator Marketing

to conduct a new market study. Through that process, Stein found a unique potential niche: a need for Sensitive Compartmented Information Facilities, a specialized area in a building to process high-level classified data.

"The federal government is kicking independent contractors out of federal facilities because there's no room for them, and independent contractors can't handle this kind of information in nonsecure facilities," Stein says.

As a result of Stein's study, the Howard County Economic Development Authority, which operates NeoTech, secured $10 million to build a second, 40,000-square-foot incubation facility that would include about 50 percent SCIF space.

"In this community, there's a lot of secure space, but most of that is fairly large and small businesses can't afford to rent it," says Vic Hess, senior vice president for small business development with HCEDA. Until the new facility is completed (in 2007 or 2008), the incubator is brokering hourly and daily rental of vacant SCIF space for its clients. "Once we build our facility, we'll have it so they can have permanent space or 'hotel' space, where they can walk in, rent it, and leave," Hess says.

That's an example of a top-down market segmentation. In top-down segmentation, you start with a broad overall market and narrow it by grouping those with similar characteristics. For example, an incubator might segment its market for potential clients by starting with all businesses in a twenty-mile radius. Segments of that market the incubator might target include start-up companies, early-stage companies, and small home-based companies. A special-focus incubator would home in even more narrowly on technology, biotech, arts, or culinary firms within those categories.

The other approach is bottom-up segmentation, in which you start with a prototype customer and match members of your overall market to that profile. For example, an incubator's prototype client might be a new company that is commercializing technology developed through or licensed from university research. Based on that profile, you would approach or accept only prospective clients that fit the description.

Bottom-up segmentation often is more efficient for incubators because the market for incubator services is relatively specialized, Smith says. "You want to make sure what the incubator has to offer matches up with what the [market segment] is seeking," she says.

For example, Cooperhouse's program at Rutgers offers "a Chinese menu of options" to food- and agriculture-based small businesses. In addition to typical incubation services such as help with business planning and marketing strategies, the program's new facility will help with food technology commercialization, market testing of new foods, and compliance with government regulations. "We will be able to help the client who needs help developing a prototype product, wants to conduct focus groups, or has to determine the shelf life of their product," Cooperhouse says. "We also can help a client who wants to use their own production site for testing."

With that lineup of services in mind, he divided New Jersey's food and agriculture industry into four categories of potential clients: farmers and cooperatives creating new value-added products; start-up food companies with differentiated products and/or new technologies to bring to market; existing small and mid-sized companies that need help with new product introductions or operations, quality assurance, and food safety issues; and retailers or restaurants that may be interested in buying local products. Each of those markets, he says, has unique needs that his program can fulfill.

A simple way to characterize your current and past clients is to ask them about themselves. New Hampshire's Gustafson includes demographic information on her client application forms. "We have their age, income, education, ethnicity," she says. She has a database of information on every Amoskeag client, past and present; with that information, she knows which radio stations to run public-service announcements on and how the incubator's client profile has changed over time.

Identifying Potential Partners and Sponsors

Getting clients in the door is paramount to your incubator's viability. But communicating only or directly to entrepreneurs won't ensure long-term success. You need support from other segments of the community, both financial and philosophical.

Forming partnerships with other businesses and organizations can be a great way to generate referrals to the incubator. Evan M. Jones, head of digital and incubation with @Wales Digital Media Initiative in Cardiff, Wales, says he would rather market his program to banks, accountants, and lawyers than to small-business owners.

"We're always asking [our clients], 'Who are you going to sell to? Who is your target really?'" Jones says. For example, he says, if you ask someone to describe the primary buyer of Heinz baked beans, they'd probably say it's a woman buying food for her family. That's wrong, Jones says; the biggest customers for Heinz baked beans are the wholesalers who supply grocery stores. "It's all effort wasted if the baked beans are not in the stores," he says. "It's about who *really* is your customer."

And in the case of an incubator, Jones says, the true customers may be the bankers, accountants, attorneys, landlords, economic developers, and others who regularly encounter entrepreneurs. They can offer a lot of bang for your marketing buck because they can refer potential clients, serve as mentors and advisors to the incubator and its clients, and sponsor the incubator or its events.

"Think of them as wholesalers of the information you need," says consultant Stein.

For example, Jones has cultivated a good working relationship with commercial landlords. "They can see us coming back with a financially stable company to occupy their premises in the not-too-distant future," he says. "We've had a number of recommendations from landlords."

Don't limit yourself to the usual suspects, either. "Look for groups in other parts of the community whose interests align and intersect with the incubator's," Smith says. An incubator's broad mission is to help create successful businesses. Who else would get a boost from having more businesses around? "In many communities, the power company is very interested in being an incubator sponsor," Smith says. "They will benefit from an increase in business activity." Similarly, real estate companies, relocation specialists, hotels, and convention centers also may be interested in working with you.

If those sectors have a trade or professional association, you can use that organization as a de facto focus group for feedback on your incubation program. Thomas has surveyed members of the Greater Baltimore Committee—a group of business, education, government, and nonprofit leaders that works to strengthen the city's economy—to gain insights into techcenter@UMBC's market. The survey brought her not only market information, but also some new friends of the incubator. The incubator twice has hosted GBC Bioscience Breakfast events and had client CEOs speak to the group. A life-science venture capitalist brought one of his partners to make a presentation at another event. "We got all of that from doing a survey of GBC members," Thomas says.

Positioning Your Program in the Local Market

Market research can help you position your incubator within the local market. To some extent, that's about knowing who else provides services to start-up and small businesses so you can explain to potential clients what your program offers their businesses that they can't get somewhere else. Knowing your competition also can help you justify your existence to sponsors and stakeholders, or tell possible partners why they should associate with your incubator.

Market position can be more complicated, though. How the community views the incubator can have a big impact on applications and referrals—and you can affect that view with something as (seemingly) simple as a name change.

Targeting Promotions to Individual Markets

Wanna make an easy $100 bucks???

Refer a new tenant to the EDC facility in St. Peters, and we'll pay you $100 when they sign a new lease between now and May 31, 2005!
Call Craig Frahm for more info at 636.441.6880, ext. 228

TAKE BACK YOUR BASEMENT OR SPARE ROOM

Now Leasing!!!
Office Suites
Warehouse & Production Space

includes front desk staff, shared office equipment, conference rooms, training programs, access to financing and counseling assistance

EDC small business incubator
5988 Mid Rivers Mall Drive
in St. Peters

636-441-6880
www.edcstcharlescounty.com

TIME IS RUNNING OUT!
No security deposit for new tenants through May 31st
offices, warehouse, production space now available for local entrepreneurs
- month-to-month leases
- front desk staff & shared office equipment
- conference rooms & loading docks
- 5988 Mid Rivers Mall Drive in St. Peters

Call Craig Frahm at
636.441.6880 x 228

Postcards reprinted with permission of the Economic Development Center of St. Charles County

To boost occupancy in its incubation facilities in 2005, the Economic Development Center of St. Charles County in St. Peters, Missouri, took a three-pronged approach. It targeted home-based businesses with a mailing and by airing a ten-minute program about the incubators on cable-TV access channels. It also homed in on start-ups with an offer to waive security deposits for new clients, and encouraged word-of-mouth referrals by paying $100 to existing clients who referred a new client. The campaign netted seventeen new clients, and both facilities have waiting lists.

When it was founded in the late 1980s, the incubator sponsored by Intelligent Systems Corp. in Atlanta, Georgia, was called the Shared Resource Technology Center. By the beginning of the dot-com boom—when incubators were springing up everywhere—the incubator's leadership thought a name change was in order. "There were all these [new] incubators with fancy names," says Executive Director Bonnie Herron. "We thought ours sounded dull."

The incubator hired a marketing firm to help it devise a new name. "They did all these exercises to help us come up with new names and did some informal surveys to see how the market perceived us," Herron says. The incubator became the Intelligent Systems Incubator "because that's how people referred to us," she says.

But what people call you and what you really are may be two different things. Over time, Herron found that having her sponsor's name in the incubator's name actually discouraged some potential clients. "It made some people not approach us because they thought [Intelligent Systems] had to own part of their company," she says. Even existing clients were reluctant to say they were in

Gauging Your Program's Reputation in the Industry

Founded in 1995, the University of Florida Sid Martin Biotechnology Incubator in Alachua, Florida, is one of the oldest biotechnology incubators in the United States. Although there are now dozens of U.S. biotech incubators, in 2000 it was still a relatively young sector. "We wanted not only to increase our visibility as a leader in this area, but also to get a better picture of where we fit into the industry and how we could collaborate with others and share information," says Incubator Manager Patti Breedlove.

The incubator contracted with Mason Strategic Communications, a Florida marketing firm that came highly recommended. In addition, "Their firm recognized that there was some growth in Florida in [biotechnology] and that it would be beneficial for them to become familiar with it, so they showed some genuine interest in the subject matter," Breedlove says.

Over the course of six months, Mason researchers called nine biotech incubators around the country. Without identifying their client, the researchers asked competitors about their programs and accomplishments, and waited to see if they would mention the Sid Martin incubator.

"One of the things that surprised us was that we were very well-known nationally in incubation," Breedlove says. "A lot of them said, 'You should call BDI in Florida; they're doing a lot,' which was kind of cool."

The researchers also found that at that point, the biotech incubation industry was still forming standards and best practices. As a result, the incubator became more aggressive in promoting itself nationally within the industry. "It encouraged us to attend NBIA meetings more regularly and to take more of a leadership role to pass our expertise on to others," says Breedlove, who has presented several sessions at NBIA conferences about biotech incubation. "We recognized that this was a young sector and that we needed to help NBIA at the national level with the development of this sector."

Taking a higher profile may have helped spur Florida's growing biotechnology cluster, particularly after the Sunshine State's tourism industry faltered in the wake of the September 11, 2001, attacks. "It was a real wake-up call to diversify our state's economy," Breedlove says. "Governor [Jeb] Bush made a decision that this was an opportunity to grow technology [companies], particularly in the life sciences. I'm sure his exposure to the growing biotechnology sector, in which we had a leadership role, played a part in that."

the Intelligent Systems Incubator because it caused confusion among their own customers about whether they were part of Intelligent Systems or an independent company.

"It became a question of, how do we position the incubator within the community and make it clearer as to who we work with and how?" Herron says.

To prepare for a third name change in 2005, Herron created a task force comprising herself, the president of Intelligent Systems, and two members of her staff, one who is in charge of the facility and another who works with clients. "When we went outside, we spent $3,000 and it came back to a decision that we would have made on our own," she says. "This time we thought, 'We're fairly creative, we can do this.'"

Members of the group researched possible names. Herron checked the NBIA member directory to see what names were popular; others checked economic development and business organizations. "We came up with this long list of typical names and combinations," Herron says. The term "innovation" came up often, so they decided that the new name should include that word. And because the incubator is located in an industrial park called Gwinnett Park, the group thought that should be included in the name as well.

Their next step was to run the name "Gwinnett Innovation Park" past current clients. "We asked them, 'Would you feel good about being associated with this name? Would you say you were in the Gwinnett Innovation Park?'" Herron says. "Everybody was very positive about it."

With that feedback, Herron took the name to a freelance graphic designer to devise a new logo and a new look for the incubator's Web site and brochure. The package was launched in conjunction with a business-plan competition called the Gwinnett Innovation Challenge. "We were able to leverage that name and the connection to us to get a little more marketing play," she says.

Another aspect of market position is ensuring that you're communicating effectively with your stakeholders. If they don't understand your program and its mission, they won't support you—and your market position will slide rapidly.

In 2006, a year after opening, the MidMichigan Innovation Center in Midland, Michigan, surveyed stakeholders from the four communities it serves. The purpose of the qualitative study was to get baseline opinions about the incubator for future satisfaction measurements, says Executive Director Donald C. Schutt.

"We just didn't feel that we could assume that we understood what the communities wanted until we asked," he says.

With the help of a local university, Schutt devised an interview script that was designed to elicit opinions about economic development in general without revealing that the incubator was behind the survey. Then, the interviewer disclosed that MMIC was the subject of the research and asked questions about the incubator.

"There's a lot of conflict in our state because of unemployment," Schutt says. "We let all these leaders tell us [what they thought] about the economy. Then we said, 'We're with the incubator, what do you think we should be doing?'"

The results were eye-opening. Of eleven interest groups surveyed, only one—entrepreneurs—understood that the incubator's mission is to bolster small-business success. "Everybody but entrepreneurs saw jobs as the primary reason for our existence," Schutt says. But it's unlikely that an incubator can match the number of jobs lost by Michigan's manufacturing base. By measuring the incubator's success purely by jobs created—rather than businesses created or tax dollars generated—some community members are missing the point of incubation, and will likely be disappointed no matter how well MMIC performs.

There are other misconceptions to overcome as well. "People did not understand that we rent at commercial rates, but that we provide a whole lot of services that our clients would normally have to pay [someone else] for," Schutt says. "Some people feel we should be giving away space at no cost to help these companies get started."

To ensure that his program retains and builds community support, Schutt will focus much of his communications on how incubation works and why.

"We have to go back and convince them that jobs are a result, not an objective" of incu-

Setting Prices for Space and Services

Market research can help you set a fair price for incubator space and services. This is important for two reasons. First, charging adequately for space and services is vital to achieving self-sustainability—the ability to cover expenses with predictable, reliable sources of funding (both internal, such as rents and fees, and external, such as grants and sponsorships). If you're charging too little, you won't make enough money to pay your bills. If you're charging too much, clients will go elsewhere for assistance. Second, an understanding of where your rent and program fees fit into the overall market will help you explain to clients why your incubation program is worth their money.

Many incubators base their rental rates on their local market. Finding that information is pretty simple: just pick up the phone. "Call a couple of commercial realtors and ask them what their rental rates are," says Charles Stein, president of Strategic Development Services, a consulting firm in Columbus, Ohio, that specializes in incubator development and funding. Commercial landlords should not consider the incubator competition, he adds: "Commercial realtors don't want to handle seven hundred square feet of space—they should refer those inquiries to the incubator," he says. "When an incubator company has blown up to ten people and needs several thousand square feet of space, there should be a commercial realtor you can hand them off to." Knowing that you're grooming future tenants should make developers happy to have you around.

Once you have an idea what local office space rents for, you can begin to calculate your own price structure. Most incubator developers and consultants advise against pegging incubator charges strictly to market rental rates because an incubator is more than a physical location; it also offers services that help young businesses grow, and your price structure should reflect that fact.

Market research can help in that regard, too. Make a list of all the services the incubator provides, from faxes and copying to business counseling and brown-bag lunch seminars. Give each a dollar value by figuring the retail cost of those same services if the client were to buy them at retail—for example, the cost of copies at FedEx Kinko's and the average hourly rates for business consulting (just call a few consultants and ask). You can use this data to set actual rates, as well as to lay out your value proposition to potential clients.

Jasper Welch, director of the San Juan College Enterprise Center in Farmington, New Mexico, checks his price points about every other year. For a few hundred dollars, he hires a consultant to call several key commercial landlords to see what their lease rates are. If market rates have gone up, Welch adjusts his fees accordingly. For example, his 2006 survey found that while the incubator's rate of $5 per square foot for industrial space was on par with local rates, its $12 per square foot for office space was a little low.

He hasn't had trouble getting information from landlords, he says. "When our incubator first started, we had a lot of criticism that we were competing with the private sector," he says. "We've pretty much put that to bed through good public relations. Now [landlords] see us spinning companies out that want to lease space [from them]."

bation, he says. "To get these communities behind us and pulling together, the first thing we have to work on is the vernacular. We have to do a better job of establishing definitions."

Fine-Tuning Your Services

Another way you can use information gathered via market research is to find out what clients want and need. And the best way to learn that is to simply ask, using a questionnaire or just taking note of what you hear in the hallways.

Clients of the Amoskeag Business Incubator complete an annual written review, which includes a request for program feedback and suggestions. In one such survey, clients asked for regular all-incubator meetings, something executive director Gustafson had resisted. "I had always felt like I didn't have time for it," she says. But she acquiesced and began offering a monthly breakfast meeting in which she talks about incubator news and policies and clients take turns making presentations about their businesses. They also talk about their successes, challenges, and various business topics; sometimes Gustafson invites an outside presenter.

The meetings created a more collegial feel within the incubator and fostered greater cooperation among clients, Gustafson says. "They've been more inclined to [work] with each other, and they talk more in the hallway," she says. "It took some of those businesses that stick more to themselves and got them out there. It's definitely had a positive impact."

She also surveyed clients about what they would like to see in the incubator's new facility, which opened in 2005. As a result of their input, she cut back on the number of office sizes available (from eight to four), added a kitchen and an extra conference room, put heavier insulation between offices to dampen noise, and allowed clients to use empty office space for storage.

"The feedback has been positive," Gustafson says. "They love the better acoustics—you can't hear what everybody else is saying. Everybody uses the kitchen and the second conference room, and probably 80 percent are using the storage room."

Just because clients ask for something, though, doesn't mean they're willing to pay for it, so be sure to give them feedback on the cost before opening your checkbook. When clients of a Midwestern technology incubator asked for a videoconferencing system, the incubator's manager complied, at a cost of several thousand dollars. But clients balked at the $125-an-hour charge for its use, even though that fee was less than what other companies in the area charged for use of their systems. "We now have the equipment stashed away in a closet," the manager says. "For us, it was a huge waste of money and taught me an expensive lesson as an incubator manager: don't believe clients really need something until they are willing to pay money for it."

Not all program changes have to be physical. Sometimes, your services may be right on the money, only your clients don't know it.

As part of an overall market survey conducted in 2000, researchers for the University of Florida Sid Martin Biotechnology Incubator in Alachua, Florida, asked clients to rank the importance of various incubator services and benefits. They then compared those ratings with the incubator's perception of their importance. The differences were sometimes startling, says Incubator Manager Patti Breedlove.

"These are generally scientist-founded companies," she says. "The biggest challenge is getting business leadership in these companies, and until then, they don't recognize the value of certain things." For example, the clients interviewed for the survey placed far less importance on some services—such as the incubator's assistance with business and financial planning, help in finding funding sources, and collaboration with the University of Florida's Office of Technology Licensing—than the incubator staff did.

The disconnect exemplified a common problem among technology incubators: researchers commercializing new technologies tend to focus more on the lab than the balance sheet. Part of the job of incubating such companies is ensuring that the scientists in charge understand that they need to develop their business skills—or recruit other individuals who have them.

"These findings reinforced our commitment to make sure that incubator management delivered that message at every turn, and to provide activities which give our start-up scientists a chance to mingle and meet with business leadership of other companies in our incubator," Breedlove says.

As a result, the incubator now hosts monthly networking socials for clients and graduates. It also does more to promote matchmaking between researchers and entrepreneurs, such as sponsoring a program through the Office of Technology Licensing that will, in some cases, pay entrepreneurs to write business plans and market assessments for scientists interested in starting a company. "The hope is that the business person and the scientist will work well together and end up starting a company together," Breedlove says.

Graduates are another good source of feedback on your program. At the Louisiana Business & Technology Center in Baton Rouge, Louisiana, Executive Director Charles D'Agostino conducts an exit interview with the principals of graduating companies. He asks them what services they valued most, what could be added or done better, and what they could have done without. "We can use this information to improve our services," D'Agostino says.

As a result of those interviews, D'Agostino implemented monthly lunches and quarterly socials for clients. "In the early days when we were small, interaction just happened," he says. "We learned that it had not been happening in recent years and that we need to be more proactive to promote interaction and the building of social and personal networks between businesses." And at the graduates' request, D'Agostino keeps them on the mailing list for the events so they can participate as well.

The Bottom Line

As you've seen from the examples in this chapter, market research practices and projects vary widely across the incubation industry. Some incubators have the resources to devote tens of thousands of dollars to in-depth, complex market surveys. Others rely on informal and inexpensive techniques to gather feedback and information.

We've said it before, but we'll say it again: you may not think you're doing market research, but you probably are. Whenever you ask your clients what services they'd like you to offer; whenever you collect contact information from community and business leaders; even if you cock an ear at a business lunch to catch a juicy bit of information—that's market research.

No matter how you do it, market research can have a big impact on your bottom line. Rutgers' Cooperhouse has set a goal of achieving self-sustainability for his new food incubation facility within three years of its opening. And he's confident he will reach it, in part because he has put a lot of time and resources into learning as much as he could about his market. "There's a high correlation between doing market research and a dramatically shorter time to sustainability," he says. "I believe we can be self-sustaining in three years or less because of the depth of our understanding of our customer base and the multiple revenue sources we've created to meet their needs."

Building and Maintaining a Marketing Database

From the old-fashioned Rolodex to complex online databases, a robust and updated list of contacts—potential and current clients, former clients and graduates, business support and economic development organizations, professionals, and political figures—can form the backbone of your marketing program. Most obviously, you can use the database to create mailing lists for incubator promotions. But you also can generate a history of the incubator's interaction with different organizations, which can help you (or your successor) get a long-term view of alliances and partnerships. Or you can analyze the types of contacts in the database to see if you're missing particular industry sectors.

To start, make sure you're capturing information from everyone who comes in contact with the incubator: inquiries from prospective clients, registrants for events and seminars, business cards collected when you speak to community organizations.

"I've got five Rolodexes on my desk," says Mark S. Long, president & CEO of the Indiana University Emerging Technologies Center in Indianapolis, Indiana. "If they're in Indiana, I know 'em."

If your incubator is new or your contact list hasn't been kept up to date, it might be worthwhile to buy a mailing list from a marketing or public relations firm. Just remember that a purchased list can be far more broad than you need; you may want to comb through it to exclude contacts that obviously won't lead to business for the incubator. For example, the NeoTech Incubator in Columbia, Maryland, buys lists from a marketing firm that tracks new business licenses issued in its region, then sends literature about the incubator to list members who clearly are technology companies. "If the business license says 'Bea's Janitorial,' they don't [send] it," says Charles Stein—president of Strategic Development Services, a consulting firm in Columbus, Ohio, that specializes in incubator development and funding—who has worked with NeoTech on marketing. "If it says 'DataTech,' they will." On the other hand, a rural incubator might be more than willing to attract a new janitorial company if it created new jobs in the region.

At the minimum, you should keep a record of the name, title, and e-mail address of the primary contacts; the name of the organization; its mailing address, telephone and fax numbers; and the organization's Web site address. The extent of other information you collect—company size, NAICS codes, history with the incubator, etc.—is up to you.

While the Rolodex has nostalgic charm, your contact list will be most useful if kept and maintained electronically. Depending on the size and extent of your list, you may keep the data in a simple spreadsheet. Database programs offer more flexibility in configuring information, allowing you to search the contents by specific criteria, such as ZIP code or contact type (client, graduate, partner) if you include a field for that data.

If your mailing list is especially large and you rely on e-mail for communications, you may want to invest in an online mailing service. Fees are usually based on the number of addresses you store; subscribers can send an unlimited number of e-mails to their list. The services also generally provide e-mail tracking tools and automatic opt-in/opt-out messages to comply with federal anti-spam regulations.

An online service also can protect your subscribers from computer viruses. Until 2005, Mildred Walters, executive director of the Nashville Business Incubation Center in Nashville, Tennessee, had been sending her incubator's e-newsletter from her own computer using Microsoft Outlook. But after unknowingly sending a computer virus along with one issue of the newsletter, she signed up with Constant Contact, one of the more popular online e-mail services. She uses it not only to distribute her newsletter, but also to send invitations and announcements.

"It's really easy to use," she says. "Everything is stable and has a professional look."

CHAPTER 2
Creating a Marketing Plan

A marketing plan is more than a map. It's a touchstone for you, your staff, and your stakeholders, a statement of what you believe your incubation program can achieve. It's a checklist of what needs to be done to attract more or better clients, and new or stronger partners and sponsors. It's a snapshot of your incubation program's potential at a particular point in time, something you can look back on to measure your progress and renew your commitment to improving your incubation program.

Sounds a bit like a business plan, doesn't it? It is—and it isn't. Your business plan describes the overall goals and benchmarks for your incubation program. The marketing plan supports your business plan as one way to achieve particular business goals.

"The business plan is the big umbrella," says Lisa S. Smith, vice president of marketing and a principal with ANGLE Technology in Charlottesville, Virginia, an international consulting firm that plans and operates incubators. "It sets the direction: what kind of structure you have, what your selection and graduation processes are, what metrics you're going to use to measure impact. The marketing plan is a subset of that. It's an engine that drives you toward the realization of your business plan's goals."

Just how elaborate your marketing plan gets is up to you. In preparing this book, NBIA requested copies of marketing plans from thirty different incubators. The plans we received ranged from a one- or two-page checklist to a twenty-page document packed with charts and tables. Many incubators include their marketing plan in their overall strategic plan. It's not important how long or detailed your plan is; what matters is that you have a usable document that outlines your marketing goals.

For example, Jasper Welch's marketing plan for the San Juan College Enterprise Center in Farmington, New Mexico, is a list of fifteen marketing strategies, all in support of the incubator's overall goals: to "educate the business, college and San Juan County communities about the benefits and goals of the business incubation program at the Enterprise Center" and "attract viable start-up companies and quality emerging companies to the Enterprise Center."

It makes for a short plan, Welch says, but it's enough for his needs—and it sets an example for clients. "When companies come in and act all brain-dead about marketing, I can whip this out and say, 'At least do this,'" he says. "It's kind of hard for us to preach the need to have a marketing plan if we don't have one. Even if it's on a shoestring, at least we have a plan."

Elements of a Marketing Plan

As noted above, working incubator marketing plans vary widely in length and detail. Most of them, however, have elements in common:

- An executive summary (usually for longer and more complex plans)
- A statement of the incubator's overall business goal or vision
- A description of the incubation program and current services
- A description of the overall market and the incubator's role in that market
- An analysis of what the incubator does well and where it can improve
- A list of specific marketing goals and strategies to achieve them
- A timeline of marketing activities, often with responsibilities assigned
- An estimate of the expected costs associated with each strategy or activity
- Some way to measure the success of marketing activities

Let's examine each of these components.

Executive summary. Start your plan with a brief overview of the plan's main points, including any particular challenges or goals. The summary is important not so much for you but for your staff, board members, partners, and sponsors—those who will want to know generally what's going on, rather than details. "You need an executive summary because a lot of time, that's the thing people really focus on," Smith says.

Vision statement. It's always a good idea to have your vision in writing to make sure everybody is on the same page. "It's good to have a longer-term marketing outlook to

---

Getting Organized With a Marketing Plan

Until 2003, Director Linda J. Clark's approach to marketing the Ohio University Innovation Center was, as she puts it, "disorganized." She had an excuse—overseeing construction of a new 36,000-square-foot facility on the university's Athens, Ohio, campus. Once that was finished, though, she knew she needed to be more disciplined in her planning.

She worked with a marketing communications consultant who also is an Innovation Center client to create a marketing plan. At the same time, another incubator client was helping her devise a strategic plan. And like a bar of chocolate accidentally dunked in peanut butter, the results were an unexpectedly tasty combination. Now, the Innovation Center's marketing plan is based on the goals set forth in its strategic plan.

"I intuitively knew what to market, but I didn't have it linked to the strategic plan," says Clark. "That made our marketing less effective."

Clark overhauls the strategic plan every other year to reflect changes in the operating environment. She also revisits both the strategic and marketing plans monthly; that way, she says, the plans remain an integral part of the center's operations, not just binders sitting on a bookshelf.

By regularly reviewing both plans, Clark can see which activities are working and which aren't. For example, she scrapped a goal to make two contacts with potential affiliates each month, because such outreach was being accomplished by other activities.

help solidify strategic thinking and challenge board-member thinking about whether this is the kind of future you'd really like," says Dar Schwanbeck, managing director of the Northern Alberta Business Incubator in St. Albert, Alberta, Canada. "It's about doing everything we can to create the future."

While NABI is a well-established incubation program—it was founded in 1989 and was NBIA's 2002 Incubator of the Year—it faces some challenges. Its existing building is more than fifty years old and too small to keep up with demand and expected future growth. As a result, NABI plans to build a larger, more modern building to house its program and meet future needs.

To prepare for that eventuality, NABI prepared a business and marketing plan in 2006 that included this vision statement:

> In the year 2007 the Northern Alberta Business Incubator Society will be operating a modern 30,000+ sq. ft. functional incubator facility that is capable of serving a variety of needs in a highly visible location that allows for expansion and partnering opportunities. … NABI will be a customer focused resource center for all businesses offering incubator services, counseling and education, networking opportunities and identification of sources of funding. … NABI will be self-sustaining with a strong partnership base. Its presence will result in a strong positive economic impact for all citizens in the region by creating economic opportunities, job growth, business development, retention and expansion.

That section, while not directly related to marketing, sets the stage for NABI's specific marketing goals and strategies, which come later in the document.

Incubator description. Many incubator marketing plans include overviews of current programs and services, as well as brief recaps of the incubators' histories. Knowing where you are and where you've been can help you decide where you want to go. "Based on our past experiences, we can likely predict what will work in the future," says Linda J. Clark, director of the Ohio University Innovation Center in Athens, Ohio.

Market description. Your incubation program does not operate in a vacuum. Forces outside the incubator—other service providers, commercial landlords, the political scene—can affect your operations. So can internal factors, such as a move to a new location or restructuring of your governing body. It's important to acknowledge those factors and their potential impact on your program

In its 2005 marketing plan, the Advanced Technology Development Center in Atlanta, Georgia, noted four existing market forces at play: skepticism of technology businesses following the dot-com bust; the difficulty technology entrepreneurs face in acquiring funding, which had led to a decrease in applications to the incubator; the presence of three other organizations that cater to technology start-ups; and a move to a larger facility in a new location. The description comprises five paragraphs in a little more than half a page, but it shows the incubator's place within the larger market and potential challenges it faces.

With those factors in mind, General Manager Tony Antoniades knew what to emphasize to potential clients: ATDC's strong reputation, its track record in linking clients to investors, and its attractive facility in the heart of Atlanta's technology community. In other words, understanding the larger market environment helped shape the program's marketing messages.

"We looked at what our strong points were, what was new that we could promote, and what entrepreneurs really needed," Antoniades says.

NABI, on the other hand, focuses on expected future population growth and a corresponding need for expanded business development services. It notes that while there are other business service providers available in its region, few have NABI's range of services or its track record, and those that do are sector-focused programs.

"The province of Alberta is among the fastest-growing jurisdictions in North America, so business start-up and growth are at all-time highs," Schwanbeck says. As the region's only mixed-use incubator, he says, NABI has to recognize what's coming and be ready to communicate its message to potential clients. "It seems that we are the only folks in the local/regional market that are trying to address the issue of improved business performance and survival" for small, nontechnology businesses, he says.

Incubator analysis. Taking a hard look at the incubation program itself can help you spot trends, identify untapped staff resources, and get ready for changes in your market. In many cases, this examination takes the form of a SWOT analysis of strengths, weaknesses, opportunities, and threats. (See "Taking a SWOT at Your Program" on page 31.)

The Canterbury Enterprise Hub in Canterbury, England, opened in January 2004. Its marketing plan for that year featured a long SWOT list that included:

- Strengths: staff experience and expertise; high-tech space and facilities; partners; good relationships with other organizations

Twenty Questions: Developing Your Marketing Focus

These twenty questions can help you get started on your marketing plan by encouraging you see your program the way your customers do. These questions focus on potential clients, but can be easily altered to apply to partners, sponsors, and stakeholders.

1. Who is your most likely client?
2. How is that potential client different from the general population?
3. What events trigger the need or desire for incubation services?
4. When does this trigger occur? Can it be predicted?
5. How does that potential client go about deciding whether to enter an incubator?
6. What are the potential client's key decision factors?
7. How do you compete with other service providers on these factors?
8. Are these differences known to the potential client?
9. Are these differences meaningful to the potential client?
10. How can your incubation program be exposed to your most likely customers?
11. What other noncompeting organizations share this target market?
12. How can you promote your incubation program to existing clients?
13. What other new services could you sell to existing clients?
14. What is your competition doing to lure potential/current clients away?
15. What are other incubators doing to increase their client base?
16. What current nonsales-producing costs can be converted into sales-producing investments?
17. What can your partners or sponsors do to help you improve your current services/awareness/occupancy?
18. What emerging social, economic, or technological trends can be turned into new client opportunities?
19. What new markets could be served with a slight modification of your current facilities and services?
20. How can you make your incubation program easier to enter or use?

- Weaknesses: organizing events; Hub not widely known; lack of marketing funds and staff; need for more complete marketing collateral
- Opportunities: planned fast train links to London and European continent; proximity to airport; tax advantages for European companies; partnerships with European universities; University of Kent plans to expand business campus
- Threats: changes in government; changes in economy; possible delays in availability of graduate space; delays in implementing/cancellation of train links; competition from other business parks and technology clusters

Lesley Anne Rubenstein, then director of the Hub, facilitated the SWOT. "It didn't take long because we had already done our homework," says Rubenstein, who is now chief executive of the Thames Innovation Centre in London, England.

For example, she talked with staff and faculty at the University of Kent, one of the incubator's sponsors, to determine the strengths of various departments. Being part of the university made her privy to information about the institution's research capabilities and facilities, Rubenstein says. She also researched market rent rates for office and laboratory space in the area, as well as the terms of leases.

Identifying weaknesses helped Rubenstein and her staff look for solutions. Some were simply a matter of time, such as the amount of time invested in organizing events.

Taking a SWOT at Your Program

Performing a SWOT (strengths, weaknesses, opportunities, threats) analysis is like conducting a focus group. You want to assemble a representative group of stakeholders and ask them what they think about the incubator.

"Put together a group of people—not just the incubator manager and staff," says Lisa S. Smith, vice president of marketing and a principal with ANGLE Technology in Charlottesville, Virginia, an international consulting firm that plans and operates incubators. "You might want to involve folks from your governing board, a client or two, a graduate if you have them, and maybe somebody who's completely outside the family to get other sorts of views."

Each year, the staff of the Advanced Technology Development Center in Atlanta, Georgia, holds an off-site meeting to plan for the coming year. One item on each year's agenda is a SWOT. "We use the results of the SWOT to determine our upcoming strategies for the year—which then dictate our marketing efforts," says General Manager Tony Antoniades.

Have some way to put everyone's suggestions on view: a chalkboard or whiteboard, or large easel pads. Designate one person to jot suggestions and thoughts onto the board or pads. Then ask the group four questions: What are our strengths as an organization? What are our weaknesses? What opportunities are there for our program? What threats to our program exist? And let the discussion begin.

"You want to have a really frank conversation—objective, with nobody feeling defensive," Smith says.

When the SWOT session is over, take the lists of comments and think about them carefully. "You have to do a little analysis," Smith says. "You have to decide, 'How strong an opportunity is this? How great a threat is that?'" Once the group has identified the top issues in each category, the incubator manager can craft a succinct description of what your incubation program is and what it can become. "You come out with a statement that says, 'We're really good with this, we have to be mindful of that, so we're going to do X,'" Smith says.

Creating a Marketing Plan

"As time went on, we got over the learning curve and it became less time-consuming—and a strength," Rubenstein says. Other weaknesses required more effort. For a few months, Rubenstein devoted half her working hours to developing the Hub's Web site. "The investment paid off as the site became a great marketing tool, as well as a good learning tool for our clients," she says.

Marketing goals and strategies. As you might expect, this is the one thing that every marketing plan shares. In some cases, this is all there is to an incubator's marketing plan. Your goals should be achievable and the strategies used to reach them should be measurable; otherwise, you're setting yourself up for failure.

The combination of marketing strategies you choose to achieve a particular goal is called the marketing mix. In traditional marketing, the marketing mix is organized around what is known as the Four Ps: price, promotion, product, and placement. While some incubator managers do use this approach—"I always fall back on the old Four Ps," Smith says—most of the plans NBIA received for this book are organized around particular marketing goals and the strategies to be used to achieve them.

Look at these goals and strategies from the marketing plan for the Nashville Business Incubation Center in Nashville, Tennessee:

1. Develop policies and tools to ensure that the Center has consistent presentation for external communications.
   a. Develop and maintain updated Web site (Monthly)
   b. Generate and disseminate an e-newsletter (Monthly)
   c. Distribute brochures with consistent message (Ongoing)
2. Promote the expertise of NBIC staff by utilizing speaking engagements and public appearances.
   a. Join two chambers of commerce and become active (By January)
   b. Join and become active members of two professional organizations (By January)
3. Develop partnerships with organizations to reach our targeted clientele.
   a. Invite bankers and other small business resources to the NBIC (Weekly)
   b. Visit resources and disseminate collateral material (Ongoing)
4. Communicate success of program graduates.
   a. Put on Web site
   b. In speeches to public

Before this plan was written for 2006-07, the incubator had relied primarily on mass-media advertising for marketing, which resulted in far too many inquiries from entrepreneurs who were either ill-prepared to start a business or didn't realize what the incubator would expect of them. "Some people want to operate a business by the seat of their pants," says NBIC Executive Director Mildred Walters, and they aren't ready or willing to take a more professional approach to their enterprise.

By focusing its marketing on bankers and business organizations, she says, the incubator is more likely to reach qualified entrepreneurs. "We selected groups we think have [access to] the kinds of clients we want," Walters says. "[We want clients] who are success-oriented and who will accept our approach to [helping them] manage their business."

Marketing calendar. Saying that you're going to do something is one thing; actually getting it done is something else. By assigning a due date to marketing tasks, you come a step closer to making it happen and ensure that your marketing activities are spread out over the year. Many plans' timelines include a person or group of people who are assigned to complete particular tasks by that deadline.

For the Ohio University Innovation Center, Clark draws up a master calendar of marketing activities each year. Some activities are monthly, such as networking lunches with area entrepreneurs and community leaders or relationship-building meetings with officials at the university. Others are spaced throughout the year: participating in trade shows, sponsoring regional events, and so on. By looking at the long-term view, Clark prevents being overwhelmed by having too much going on at once.

The activities are listed under each month's heading with a check-off box. "It's like a to-do list," Clark says. "That breaks the marketing down into pieces that are manageable."

While your marketing calendar may cover a twelve-month period, that isn't to say that you shouldn't change your plan more frequently. "Your plan really should be full of ideas, and you should never be afraid to add or subtract things as the market changes," Smith says. "If a local plant is closing and you don't have outreach to that community, you should. It's a living, breathing document and you're tinkering with it all the time. It has to remain relevant and current."

Budget. You don't need to have a formal budget for your plan—in many cases, the marketing plans received for this book simply assigned a dollar amount alongside each strategy—but you do need to have some sense of what your marketing activities are going to cost. Your marketing budget, naturally, will depend on balancing what you want to do versus what you can afford. Some incubation programs with extensive sponsorships spend tens of thousands of dollars on marketing; others are lucky to have $500 a year to devote to marketing.

"If you're a program within a bigger organization, you usually have a budget [from them], so you have a vague sense of what you have to work with. If that's not the case, try to look at what is the absolute minimum you need to do ... to accomplish your job," Smith says. "It's not always a good idea to say, 'I have $50,000, what can I do with it?'"

When she was preparing a marketing plan for the BioAccelerator, a life science incubator ANGLE manages in Fairfax County, Virginia, Smith made a list of the things she needed: a logo, a Web site, a brochure, a folder, and a template for a PowerPoint presentation. She took that list to an advertising and public relations firm and asked for estimates on each item. "I could then go to my boss and say, 'I've talked with this firm and received a ballpark estimate, and this is going to cost X amount of money,'" she says. "I highly recommend that approach. It gave me, my boss, and our client a lot of confidence."

When preparing your marketing budget, consider the entire spectrum of marketing strategies. You're probably already spending money on activities that you don't consider to be marketing, but actually serve or support

Try Something Different

The Louisiana Business & Technology Center in Baton Rouge, Louisiana, promotes its program and clients with trading-style cards that are given out at trade shows and to community leaders, service providers, and potential clients. The front shows a picture of a client's product or service; the back features information about LBTC. "We receive great comments about the cards, and people are more likely to keep them on their desk than regular brochures," says Executive Director Charles D'Agostino. He pays less than $2,000 for 2,500 sets of sixteen full-color cards.

that purpose. For example, Mark Lieberman, administrator of the Business Technology Center of Los Angeles County in Altadena, California, doesn't include a marketing line item in his budget. "I'm a government-based incubator, and governments don't spend money on marketing," he says. (His incubation program is a project of the Community Development Commission of Los Angeles County, where Lieberman is manager of regional economic development.)

But his budget does cover his $800 membership in ProVisors, a national networking group for senior professionals. Though pricey, "It's well worth it," he says. Through that membership, Lieberman makes contacts with attorneys, CPAs, marketing consultants, and others who can benefit his program and his clients as mentors and speakers. He also does a lot of speaking to community groups and at colleges and universities. "People hear about us, and that's my marketing," he says.

What you can put in your budget may be limited by law or policy. Because it is part of a publicly funded college, the San Juan College Enterprise Center in Farmington, New Mexico, can't use any of its $6,000 marketing budget for promotional items or to wine and dine potential partners. "We can't use public funds for private purposes, so I can't give you a shirt or take you to lunch," says Director Jasper Welch. "And we don't have much in the way of imprinted items."

Instead, he splurges on pictures. About every eighteen months, Welch hires a professional photographer to shoot high-quality images of the incubator and its clients. The photos appear in the incubator's brochure, on its Web site, in ads placed in the local business journal, and as illustrations with press releases. "It's been really helpful," he says.

Your marketing budget may change from year to year depending on your situation. When the Amoskeag Business Incubator in Manchester, New Hampshire, split from Southern New Hampshire University—which handled much of its marketing—and moved into a new facility in 2005, Executive Director Julie Gustafson beefed up her marketing budget. What had been a $200 line item annually jumped to $2,500 in the first year of the incubator's independent existence. Not only did she have to absorb expenses the university had covered, such as postage, but also she had a larger facility. "We [were] being more aggressive because we [were] trying to fill the incubator," she says.

The extreme jump in budget was necessitated by the need to design and print new brochures, reformat the newsletter, and revamp and expand the incubator's Web site, as well as underwrite several events to promote the incubator. With those one-time costs out of the way, Gustafson says, "the marketing budget will be more like $500."

"Once it's filled we won't have to be as aggressive," she says. "We will never abandon marketing, but we will not have what we [had] going on [that] year."

And don't forget to call upon your stakeholders for help; they can be a valuable source of assistance because they want to see the incubator succeed. For example, when Los Angeles' Lieberman wanted to start an e-mail newsletter, he invited the head of a local e-marketing firm to join his board of advisors. "I offered him access to our companies; he's providing free e-mail marketing in exchange," Lieberman says. "We do the e-mails, he has the engine behind it. He gets to say he's working with Los Angeles County." And Lieberman gets his e-newsletter distributed for free.

Measuring effectiveness. Clearly, marketing requires effort and expense, so you will want to know that you're getting a good return on your investment of time and money. "I always like to be thinking, 'What are the metrics to measure the effectiveness of the marketing plan?'" Smith says. "We always consider that up front as we're designing activities: how are we going to assess performance?"

One of the simplest ways to measure effectiveness is to keep records of the sources of inquiries about the incubator. Always ask callers, visitors, and other contacts how they heard about your program. The results may surprise you. Just ask Gustafson. The Amoskeag Business Incubator keeps a book by the telephone with sheets to record the name, organization, and phone number of everyone who calls, as well as how they heard about the incubator.

"I wouldn't have known without putting together that [information] that a lot of our referrals came from our tenants and the SBDC," she says. Knowing who's making referrals—and who isn't—can show you where to concentrate your marketing. "If we're not getting referrals from them, we need to reconnect better with them," Gustafson says.

Even informal measures can provide feedback. "If I go to a conference in Estonia, we look at what [inquiries] come in the months after that," says Evan M. Jones, head of digital and incubation with @Wales Digital Media Center in Cardiff, Wales.

Charles F. D'Agostino, executive director of the Louisiana Business & Technology Center in Baton Rouge, Louisiana, doesn't track responses formally. But he knows when LBTC has made the news. "Every time we hit the Sunday paper or the business paper with a story about one of our tenants or a press release, we get a flurry of phone calls," he says.

Good record-keeping can show patterns in the effect of your marketing. For example, you might keep a database showing the date you mailed a press release and to which media outlets; which of those media outlets used the information and when; and the number of calls or Web hits you received in the days or weeks afterward. By analyzing this data over time, you might find that a particular newspaper never uses your press releases; you could meet with the editor to find out why. Or you might see that press releases on some topics generate more inquiries than others; you might decide to stop sending some press releases and increase others.

Depending on the goal, you may need to undertake some market research to measure your success. For example, if one of your goals is to increase referrals from incubator clients and graduates, you might need to survey your clients about their experiences in the incubator—after all, if they're dissatisfied, they're not going to recommend the incubator to others.

Measuring effectiveness regularly makes your marketing plan a constant part of your business operations. "If you write a plan and put it in a drawer, that's the kind of marketing success you're going to have," Smith says.

Defining Your Value Proposition

Your value proposition is the sum of everything you have to offer a client, partner, or sponsor. "You have to think of the total package you're giving," says Robert Hisrich, Garvin Professor of Global Entrepreneurship and director of the Thunderbird Global Incubator at the Thunderbird School of Global Management in Glendale, Arizona. "Clients aren't just buying a conference room or your capabilities or your access to capital."

Defining your value proposition is key to producing a workable and effective marketing plan. Knowing exactly what it is you have to offer to potential clients and stakeholders—and aligning your offering with their needs and expectations—will help you sharpen your message and ensure that you can deliver the goods without going broke or losing credibility.

"Whatever services you're providing, that's your offering," Hisrich says. "Related to that is how much you charge, accessibility, and how you're going to promote it."

Your value proposition should be based on an analysis of internal factors (those the incubator can control, such as services and amenities) and external factors (for example, the needs and expectations of potential clients and stakeholders).

Start by taking stock of your incubation program as a whole: the facility, the services, the staff. How do you create value for a particular target market? Do you have a good location, a well-equipped building, free and plentiful parking? What benefits do you offer in terms of services—from copies and faxing to mentoring and access to capital? What kinds of expertise does your staff bring to the table? And how do all of these compare to other sources of business space and support in your area?

Next, think about a target market, such as potential clients. How do they measure value—by price, by cost/benefit ratio, by prestige? How does your offering meet their needs and expectations? How can you differentiate your offering from other resources in that potential client's eyes? How will you back up your claims? And how can you make your offering even better, either in terms of cost or in quality (or both)?

In classic marketing practice, you would boil all of that information down into a few words or sentences that encapsulate your incubation program's offering in terms that appeal to your markets' needs. "The value proposition is aimed at a particular audience, so it's expressed in slightly different ways," says Lisa S. Smith, vice president of marketing and a principal with ANGLE Technology in Charlottesville, Virginia, an international consulting firm that plans and operates incubators. Potential clients, for example, want to know how you can help them grow their businesses, so your value proposition to them might mention the staff's expertise and the program's ties to service providers. Potential sponsors, on the other hand, will want to know how you can help them achieve their own missions, such as job creation or industry sector growth; your value proposition to them would describe how your incubator bolsters those missions.

On its Web site, TechColumbus (formerly the Business Technology Center) in Columbus, Ohio, lists four separate value propositions for its primary stakeholders: entrepreneurs (what the program calls "visionaries"), private stakeholders, investors, and public partners:

Visionaries: TechColumbus can increase the probability of realizing your vision and accelerating its growth into a sustainable business.

Private Stakeholders: TechColumbus offers a unique opportunity to build collaborative relationships with companies and technologies that will shape the growing tech sector in Columbus and in Ohio.

Investors: TechColumbus offers access to early-stage investment opportunities by identifying, assessing and accelerating the growth of technology-based investable businesses.

Public Partners: By accelerating the formation of new, technology-based businesses, TechColumbus plays an essential role in the growth of Ohio's economy and the creation of high-value, high-wage jobs.

"As we go out and promote our [program], we determine what's important to our constituents," says Steven Clark, vice president of business incubation services for TechColumbus. "Our message has to be clear: that we're providing value to them individually." Being able to communicate how TechColumbus meets each audience's needs makes the incubator's overall marketing efforts more effective, he says.

Whatever your audience, though, your value proposition should be clear and unique. "Most people and companies have lousy value propositions," writes sales consultant Jill Konrath, author of *Selling to Big Companies* (Kaplan Business, 2005). "Often they're simply a description of the offering's features or capabilities. Or they're filled with self-aggrandizing puffery."

A great value proposition, Konrath says, uses hard facts. "By including specific numbers or percentages you get the decision maker's attention even faster," she writes. So instead of "Our program helps entrepreneurs succeed by providing a range of support services," you might try "Because we helped them connect with angels and venture capitalists, our clients earned $15 million in investments last year" or "With the guidance of our staff of former entrepreneurs, our graduates have made strong contributions to the area's economy, creating 150 jobs with an average salary of $45,000—15 percent higher than the area's average."

Even if you don't draft a formal value proposition statement, this analysis will help you in writing a marketing plan because it creates a complete list of everything you have to offer; in comparing your offering with your target market's needs and expectations, you can see what that market values most and thus bring that to the fore in your marketing.

"You have to think of [everything] in a strategic way," Hisrich says. "It's the entire thing you're going to give that's important."

TechColumbus in Columbus, Ohio, reached out to the city's business community with a twenty-page full-color insert in *Business First,* a local business newspaper. TechColumbus secured major corporate sponsorships to pay for the costs of design and production of the insert. "We continue to get requests and hear from people who read it," says Tim Haynes, vice president for member services and marketing at TechColumbus.

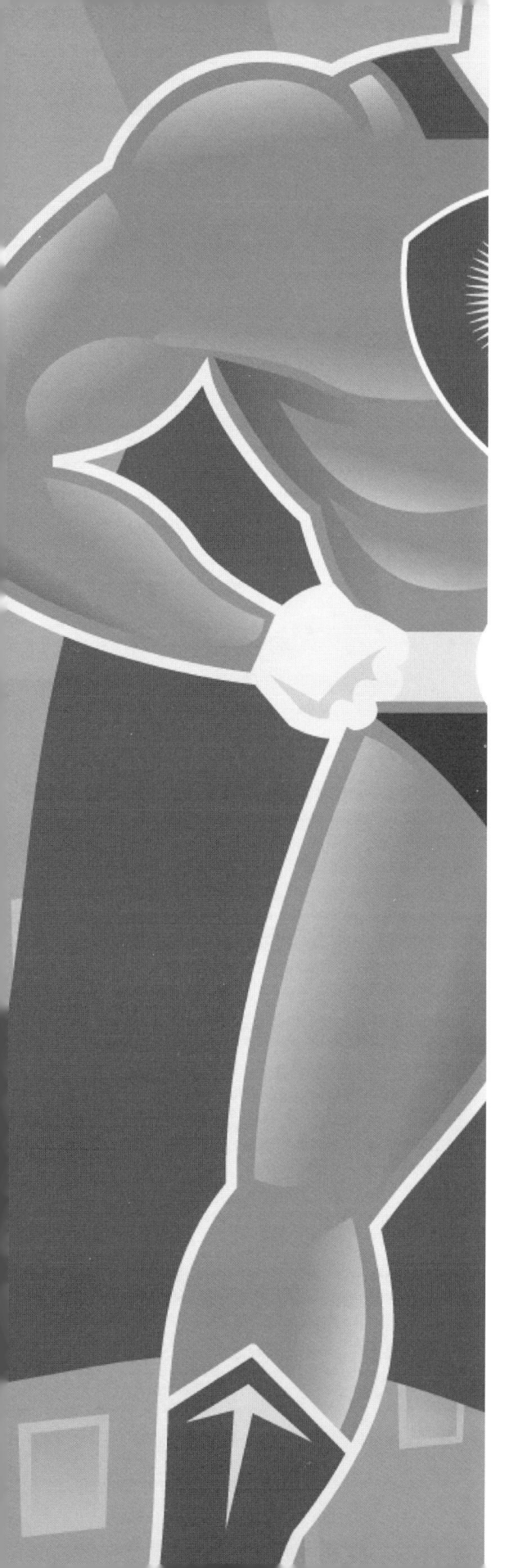

CHAPTER 3
Marketing Methods

Before we get into the good stuff, let's face the obvious: marketing an incubation program is not the same as marketing soap or software.

A basic challenge in incubator marketing is the fact that to the public at large, an incubator is still a place where chickens hatch eggs. "Getting people to understand incubation is the most difficult thing," says Evan M. Jones, head of digital and incubation with @Wales Digital Media Initiative in Cardiff, Wales. "Once people hear what we do, they get it and they're keen, but we do have to explain ourselves on a regular basis."

Part of the difficulty in explaining business incubation is that an incubator is a combination of the tangible (your facility) and the intangible. Your marketing efforts have to address not only the space clients can occupy in the incubator, but also the services you provide and the expertise of the incubator staff, among other factors.

"You have to be very specific about your unique selling propositions, what you're going to offer," says Robert Hisrich, Garvin Professor of Global Entrepreneurship and director of the Thunderbird Global Incubator at the Thunderbird School of Global Management in Glendale, Arizona. By describing exactly what the incubator offers—for example, administrative support, mentoring, access to a network of service providers—and how that helps small businesses succeed, you can "make this intangible thing called an incubator as tangible as possible," Hisrich says.

Branding Your Incubator

No matter which marketing method you choose, it should communicate your incubator's brand. At heart, a brand is a promise—of quality, of integrity, of efficiency, or whatever you want your incubator to stand for. The image you project and the reputation you build and maintain will have a big impact on the number and quality of potential clients, the number of referrals you receive from other service providers, and your ability to forge effective partnerships and sponsorships.

"Branding an incubator is not any different than branding anything," Hisrich says. "We want to establish [the incubator] just like Procter & Gamble wants to establish ... Tide."

A brand carries implications beyond the purpose of the product itself. When it markets Tide, Procter & Gamble is promoting more than clean clothes; it's selling cleanliness. A cosmetics company like Avon appeals to its customers' desire for beauty with makeup and skin-care products. You can think of your incubation program's marketing goals in the same way: incubators sell entrepreneurial success, not just space and services.

One of the first steps in communicating your brand is your incubator's name. "We want our tenants to always think globally in terms of where they're headed in the future," Hisrich says—which is why his incubator's name includes the word "global."

An established incubator may change its name to reflect a redirection in focus or a new partnership, or to better represent its location. For example, in 2005, the former Intelligent Systems Incubator in Atlanta, Georgia, became the Gwinnett Innovation Park to make it easier to attract clients. "As the Gwinnett Innovation Park, it's a lot easier for the chamber of commerce and others to remember that this is a resource for all Gwinnett County companies and entrepreneurs," says Bonnie Herron, executive director.

What's in a Name?

The name of a business incubation program can say a lot about its audience, its focus, and its mission—all of which are key in branding and marketing.

Many incubator names are straightforward; the Central Valley Business Incubator in Fresno, for example, is exactly what it says: a business incubator serving California's Central Valley region. Same goes for the Toronto Business Development Centre, located in Toronto, Ontario, Canada. These names imply a no-nonsense, taking-care-of-business atmosphere that entrepreneurs of all backgrounds might find appealing.

A name can telegraph the incubator's industry niche. The Environmental Business Cluster in San Jose, California, focuses on environmentally friendly enterprises. Urban Ventures, of Providence, Rhode Island, promotes the growth and development of small businesses in depressed urban areas. And there's little mistaking what kinds of businesses are nurtured at the Arts Incubator of Kansas City, Missouri, or Mi Kitchen es su Kitchen in New York, New York.

Other incubator names pay homage to the program's sponsor: Panasonic Tech Collaboration Group of San Jose, California, or the YWCA of Delaware Microenterprise Program in Wilmington, Delaware.

A name might combine any of these approaches. The UConn Technology Incubation Program in Storrs, Connecticut, identifies not only its focus, but also its sponsor, the University of Connecticut.

Some incubator names are plays on words. Schenectady, New York, has the U-Start Business Incubator; Dunedin, New Zealand, hosts the Upstart Business Incubator (a program of the Upstart Incubator Trust).

Then there are the names that are just ... cool. Consider Technium, in Swansea, Wales. Or InNOVAcorp, in Halifax, Nova Scotia, Canada. Or i.lab in Toowong, Queensland, Australia.

And just as there are trends in baby names, there are trends in incubator names. More than 130 of NBIA's 1,700-plus members have the word "incubator" or "incubation" in their names. But there's an up-and-comer closing in: "innovation," which shows up in more than sixty NBIA member program names.

Bonnie Herron's program dumped "incubator" (as in the Intelligent Systems Incubator in Atlanta, Georgia) in 2005, renaming itself the Gwinnett Innovation Park. "Who wouldn't want to be associated with innovation?" she says.

Likewise, the Small Business Accelerator of the Mason Enterprise Center in Fairfax, Virginia, shed its long moniker for the simpler Fairfax Innovation Center. "The old name said nothing about our sponsors," says Director Judith Barral. "The new name highlights the sponsorship of the city of Fairfax."

Selecting a name isn't as easy as it sounds. When the Business Incubator of the Greater Reston Area Chamber of Commerce in Reston, Virginia, decided to go for a shorter, catchier name in 2005, it was a group effort. "We invited lots of people to put in their suggestions: the board, the staff, the clients, our graduates," says Executive Director Stuart Miller. Miller and the board had set criteria; the new name had to identify the program as an incubator, be concise and self-explanatory, and indicate the program's quality.

Even with those limitations, the group came up with a long list of possibilities. "Ninety-eight percent of them we couldn't use because others had them," Miller says. And none of the remaining choices appealed. "For two or three months we were sort of scratching our heads," he says.

The eventual choice came from a brainstorm Miller had. "One day I was sitting at my desk thinking, 'I need an inspiration here,'" he says. "It occurred to me that INC.*spire* was close to inspiration and has 'inc' for incubator. We put a period in it because we're a technology incubator, which may be corny." Thus the program became INC.*spire*.

Most incubators have a logo that goes on business cards, letterhead, their Web sites, and other publications. More often than not, creating a logo will require the services of a professional graphic designer, who can translate your incubator's name and mission into an appealing, eye-catching image. "You want to give a good public presence to the world," says Mark S. Long, president & CEO of the Indiana University Emerging Technologies Center in Indianapolis, Indiana. "The companies coming into the building want to look professional, so I want to look professional."

In the months before the IUETC opened in 2003, Long turned to a professional public relations firm for help with marketing materials. "We told them that we needed collateral—flyers, brochures, description-type things—but also an identity, a logo that expressed what we do," Long says.

The incubator is a program of the Indiana University Research & Technology Corp. (a nonprofit agency that handles IU's technology commercialization and economic development functions), so Long wanted a logo that tied his program visually to IURTC. And since the incubator focuses on technology, the logo had to represent that sector.

The firm's designers took the IURTC logo—a red-and-black design reminiscent of DNA—and used the same colors and some graphic elements to form IUETC's logo. "They did a really good job," Long says.

You may choose to accentuate your name and logo with a tagline, a kind of motto that further projects your desired image. A good tagline is short, easily understood, and representative of your product. Avoid generic and trite phrases; think of all the cities that promote themselves with "City X Means Business." Because it's generic (what does it mean to "mean business"?) and overused, that particular tagline does little to differentiate City X from City Y. A great tagline, on the other hand, can become synonymous with your program; think of Coca-Cola and "The Real Thing," or the Yellow Pages and "Let your fingers do the walking."

The Amoskeag Business Incubator in Manchester, New Hampshire, reinforces its brand as a driver of small business success with its tagline, "Venture Forward." The motto grew out of the incubator's need to create a new identity separate from Southern New

Marketing Mistakes to Avoid

While every marketing method has its own pitfalls, there are some overall traps to avoid.

- **Information overload.** "People aren't looking for total knowledge right away," says Robert Hisrich, Garvin Professor of Global Entrepreneurship and director of the Thunderbird Global Incubator at the Thunderbird School of Global Management in Glendale, Arizona. "When your message needs to be appealing, it needs to be shortened significantly."
- **Hit-and-run marketing.** "Repetition is important," Hisrich says. "People need to be hit over the head." For example, it's better to run four quarter-page ads than a single full-page ad so readers see it more often and remember it. Select a powerful message and stick with it.
- **Unrealistic expectations.** If your incubator has been at half capacity, don't expect it to be full as soon as you start marketing. "Marketing is not a fast process," says Mark Lieberman, administrator of the Business Technology Center of Los Angeles County in Altadena, California. "To do it right takes time." Give yourself at least six months to a year to see real results.

Hampshire University, which sponsored the incubator until 2005. A marketing company devised a new logo and brainstormed several possible taglines (pro bono, of course). "We all instantly liked 'Venture Forward,'" says Executive Director Julie Gustafson. They liked the play on venture—which can mean a business or a risky journey—and how the term "forward" blended with the incubator's new logo, which uses a series of increasingly larger ovals that suggest movement. "Our mission is to help businesses move forward," she says. "We all thought 'Venture Forward' was appropriate."

However you choose to express your brand, your actions have to back up the promise implicit in your brand. If your chosen brand image is friendly, helpful service, make sure you, your staff, and your partners are actually friendly and helpful.

The Louisiana Business & Technology Center at Louisiana State University in Baton Rouge, Louisiana, has built a reputation as the place to get answers about business and economic development in the state. To Executive Director Charles F. D'Agostino, that's as simple as making sure that every call gets returned, "even if it's just to say, 'I can't do that,'" he says. "The worst thing that can happen is that a message gets lost on somebody's desk."

From your actions to your identity, communicate your brand consistently and often. Establishing a brand takes repetition, Hisrich says. "If you have pens you're giving away, that [name or logo] needs to be there. If you're doing ads, that needs to be in bolder type. On your application forms, it has to be in big type," he says. "Everything should have that brand on it."

Selecting Marketing Methods

What follows in this chapter are descriptions of the vehicles you can use to communicate your brand to your chosen target markets. So how do you decide which of these methods to use? Well, in May 2006, Angelou Economics, an economic development consulting firm based in Austin, Texas, surveyed economic development organizations across the United States about their marketing practices. Tools respondents rated as "most effective" included Web sites, cooperative marketing with a partner or sponsor, and public relations. Those rated as "moderately effective" included trade shows, special events, e-newsletters, and advertising. Telemarketing and CD-ROMs were ranked as least effective.

But marketing guru Jay Conrad Levinson would disagree. "Choose as many as you can do well," Levinson writes in *Guerrilla Marketing*. Then, he says, keep track of what works and what doesn't. If a particular method is working well, do more of it. If something isn't working, see if you can fine-tune your approach to get better results. If that doesn't work, quit using that method.

What works for one audience may not work for another. The best way to reach prospective clients may not be such a good approach for communicating with partners or sponsors. For optimum results, match your method to your market.

Advertising

Advertising is any activity in which you pay to deliver a promotional message and you are identified as the sponsor of the message. As such, advertising encompasses not only the familiar newspaper or magazine display ad, but also vehicles such as signs, banners, T-shirts, and giveaway items like pens or computer mouse pads.

Media advertising. Traditional advertising has some disadvantages, such as information overload. "People are inundated with ads again and again and again, particularly in mass media like newspapers and radio," Hisrich says. "We're just saturated." What's more, advertising can be expensive. A single newspaper or magazine ad can cost hundreds or even thousands of dollars in design and fees—and to be effective, ads have to be repeated frequently and consistently.

There are ways to make media advertising work for you, though. It's a good way to reach new audiences, raise awareness of your program, and promote your clients. And you can sometimes reduce the cost of advertising—even get it for free—through partnerships and savvy purchasing.

When The New Century Venture Center in Roanoke, Virginia, wrote a grant to launch a new program aimed at home businesses in 2003, President Lisa Ison made sure the proposal included funding for promotion. To make the most of the funding, she turned to Access, a 1999 NCVC graduate (and 2002 NBIA Outstanding Incubator Client) that had become one of Roanoke's leading advertising firms.

Working with an incubator graduate was especially helpful, Ison says. "We didn't have to explain [incubation] to them," she says. "They knew what we were about."

Ison met with the Access team to discuss the new Venture Out program, then let the firm handle the rest. "They did their creative thing with it," she says. The ads caught readers' eyes with large, offbeat photographs and headlines that captured some of the pitfalls of a home-based business. One example: "It's bad when someone at your business makes advances toward a client. It's worse when it's your dog." Each ad carried a tagline—"If you own a home-based business, isn't it time you ventured out?"—and touted NCVC's amenities and track record, along with a list of services available through the Venture Out affiliate program. Access also developed radio spots that aired on a local Christian radio station that was popular among the incubator's key 25–40 age group.

Without the grant, the ad campaign would not have been possible, Ison says. "It was very expensive," she says. She's not kidding: Although Access charged about half its going rate, it still billed for $8,600 for all its creative work; the radio ad placements cost $1,500; and the newspaper ad space came to $345. "We typically don't have the money to do that," she says.

The campaign did lead to some new full-time clients, Ison says. But its greater impact was in raising awareness of the incubator, particularly in connection with a visually appealing ad campaign. "It got a lot of attention," she says. "Everyone who saw it was like, 'Wow!'" The campaign also won an American Advertising Award from the local chapter of the American Advertising Federation.

Based on her experience with Access, Ison recommends taking on an ad agency as a client if possible. "Most [graduates] will give you a good price and good service because it's a way to give back to the incubator," she says.

Graduates aren't the only source of advertising help. With funding from Corning Inc., Alfred University, and Corning Enterprises, the Ceramics Corridor Innovation Centers—two technology incubators in southern New York state—created a thirty-second public service announcement that ran sixteen times on the Golf Channel and one hundred times on local stations during the LPGA Corning Classic in May 2005. The ads highlighted the centers' ability to help start-up companies research, develop, and bring to market new technologies. Although he won't say how much the ads cost, Executive Director Jon M. Wilder confesses that they were "very expensive" and that without corporate and institutional sponsorship, he could not have afforded them.

"It gave us exposure and awareness of our program not only nationally, but internationally," he says. Many people have told Wilder they learned about the centers from the spots, and several prospects applied to be clients.

"We think it was very successful," Wilder says. In fact, there may be more ads in the centers' future. "I'm not sure exactly when, but I believe we will continue to use TV to assist us," Wilder says.

The CCIC example is unusual; most incubators won't have such opportunities, and that's not a problem, Hisrich says. Not only

Harnessing the Power of Testimonials

For many incubator managers, the best advertising is free. "There is no better advertising than an endorsement," says Charles F. D'Agostino, executive director of the Louisiana Business & Technology Center in Baton Rouge, Louisiana. Testimonials from clients and graduates and word-of-mouth recommendations carry a lot of weight with potential clients, he says, because they come from peers. "If you're thinking of joining a gym, you might see a number of posters that say 'Come to Joe's Gym.' But if one of your friends says, 'I just joined a new gym that's superb,' you're more likely to do that than something you saw on a billboard."

Testimonials have been one of the most effective ways to recruit new clients of the Applied Process Engineering Laboratory in Richland, Washington. "That's one of the most effective things we do to get people's interest," says Charles Allen, former APEL director.

It's easy to get testimonials, says Lou Cooperhouse, director of the Rutgers Food Innovation Center in New Brunswick, New Jersey. When a client compliments you on your services or a training event participant gushes about the program, ask them to put it in writing. "Some people are so excited, you can ask them to write a testimonial about the seminar or what we've done for them," he says. "They're more than happy." Cooperhouse puts testimonials he collects on his Web site and even turns them into an appendix when he applies for grants.

is TV advertising expensive, it also reaches a much broader audience than necessary, a phenomenon he calls waste exposure. The additional expense probably won't pay off in a proportionate number of prospective clients or stakeholders, he says. "Given the cost of television advertising and its waste exposure, unless it is free, I do not think it is cost effective for an incubator," Hisrich says.

Print advertising can have the same waste-exposure drawback. You can minimize that problem by using advertising to promote your clients as well as the incubator—and including the ads in your value proposition. At the Northeast Indiana Innovation Center in Fort Wayne, Indiana, President & CEO Karl R. LaPan devotes $35,000 of his $1.25 million annual budget to advertising, nearly all of which is dedicated to promoting his clients. "The more we market our clients, the more people realize what the center does," LaPan says. "The ads put a human face on the center and [show] why we're different from traditional landlords."

Although $35,000 is a lot of money, LaPan makes it stretch by buying ad space in bulk—a year's worth in advance—and negotiating discounted rates (about half the retail rate) with four area business publications and the regional National Public Radio affiliate. "At retail, we'd pay higher rates, but we're able to get reduced rates because we're a community nonprofit creating jobs and businesses, and people share our vision," he says.

He puts those discounts to good use. Every new client receives a full-page "Innovation Spotlight" ad that uses a question-and-answer format to introduce the business and its concept. The following month, the client gets another full-page, full-color ad. "Frequency makes a difference," LaPan says.

When there are no new clients to promote, LaPan rotates full-page ads among the center's existing clients. Each client also gets a month of promotions on the local National Public Radio affiliate on a rotating basis.

"The clients appreciate that we do this, because if they were to buy that kind of advertising, it would be very expensive," LaPan says. He doesn't charge the cost of the ads back to the client through their service fees, but instead covers them through grants and his operating budget.

Of course, it's not entirely about the clients; every print ad includes the incubator's logo, and the radio ads mention the incubator as well. LaPan chooses the publication in which the ad will appear, "based on the coverage and visibility needs of the center and my thoughts and opinions on the best coverage for the clients," he says. "I also may try to integrate ads thematically, based on the editorial calendar of the given publication."

Clients are responsible for the content of their own ads, although LaPan reserves the right of final approval. And if a client's ad isn't up to snuff or the client misses the deadline, LaPan has a supply of stock ads for the center to call on. "We always have an ad ready to go," he says.

While not every incubator can devote so much money to advertising, LaPan says it pays off for him. "In a community where there's a huge vacancy rate, we have to drive value and differentiate ourselves" from commercial landlords, he says.

Linda J. Clark, director of the Ohio University Innovation Center in Athens, Ohio, says public radio and television are the most cost-effective places for broadcast ads. She spends $5,000 annually as a sponsor of WOUB Radio and WOUB-TV, the public broadcasting services of Ohio University. "We couldn't afford [these ads] if we had to rely on commercial radio and TV stations," she says.

A $3,500 sponsorship of the NPR station gets her ten fifteen-second mentions of her incubator and/or her clients every week throughout the year. The spots run during *Morning Edition* and *All Things Considered*, NPR's morning and afternoon news shows. She pays another $1,500 a year for eight fifteen-second mentions of the incubator every Wednesday between broadcasts of *The State of Ohio*, a state news program, and *NewsHour with Jim Lehrer*, PBS' nightly newscast.

The sponsorships are cost-effective because they buy continuous advertising for the incubator and its clients, Clark says. "It doesn't do any good to place an ad in the paper or on TV once or twice a year," she says. "You never know when a potential client will be [hearing] or reading about your program."

Sponsoring public radio and TV has generated business for her clients, and public broadcasting's reputation reflects well on the incubator, she says. "People tell me that they have heard and seen the sponsorships," she says. "They provide a sense of validity to our clients and program."

Of course, if you're lucky, you might even get client advertising for free. Clients of the Central Valley Business Incubator in Fresno, California, have quarterly chances to get free radio and print ads through a scholarship program. Each quarter, KJWL, a locally owned station in Fresno, gives two scholarships, worth $2,500 and $1,000 apiece, for sixty-second commercials. *The Business Journal*, also in Fresno, offers $2,500 worth of advertising to a CVBI client each quarter.

The program began in 2003, when KJWL approached the incubator to offer its services. That contact came in response to public speaking engagements about the incubator, says Kelli Furtado, the incubator's former chief operating officer. "Once the radio station got involved, we mentioned the project to *The Business Journal* and they matched it," she says.

The work on the incubator's end is minimal. "We simply invite our clients to apply, and then we forward the applications to the advertisers to make their selection of the winner," Furtado says. The radio station and newspaper work with the client to develop an ad. In a further donation, the ad is then turned over to the client company, which can run it on other stations or in other publications, Furtado says.

The ads don't have to mention the incubator, but that is changing, Furtado says. The incubator is working with the advertisers to mention CVBI without interfering too much with the client's ad—using an introductory tagline on the radio and a header for the print ads, she says.

Other forms of advertising. There's more to advertising, though, than newspapers and radio. Perhaps the most effective—and easily overlooked—is signage. Just ask Ed Hobbs, general manager of the Toronto Business Development Centre in Toronto, Ontario, Canada. The incubator is located on one of the city's busiest streets, but only one side of the building—the east—had a

---

Wearing a Logo on Your Sleeve

Every year, the Advanced Technology Development Center in Atlanta, Georgia, produces a T-shirt bearing the names and logos of all current clients on the back, the ATDC logo on the front, and the name and logo of the T-shirt sponsor on the sleeve. "I want to get enough out there that I'll be at the grocery store and see somebody wearing one," says General Manager Tony Antoniades.

T-shirt shown with permission of the Advanced Technology Development Center; photo by Suzanne Burkey

sign. Anyone approaching the building from another direction had no idea what it was. When the time came to paint the facility's interior, Hobbs got the contractor to paint the program's name and logo on each side of the building's exterior. The result: walk-in traffic tripled in one year.

Signs don't have to be permanent to be effective, though. The Amoskeag Business Incubator is located right next to Manchester's Fisher Cats Stadium, home of a AA professional baseball team. The stadium, which opened in 2005, seats 6,500 and hosts nearly one hundred home games from April to September. For about $150, manager Gustafson had a giant banner made with the incubator's name on it. With her landlord's blessing, she hangs the banner on the side of the building facing the ballpark during every Fisher Cats home game. And because many people park in the area for events and concerts at the nearby civic center, Gustafson makes sure the banner is displayed for them, too.

"We got the idea because a couple of other tenants [in the building] hang banners outside when they are having special sales, plus we noticed that several hundred people were walking past the building," she says. "It just made sense."

The banner also gets used at incubator events and at trade shows Gustafson attends. While the banner hasn't generated lots of client traffic, she says it was worth the investment anyway. "It helps with branding and awareness," she says.

Another way to get your incubator's name in front of lots of people is swag—giveaway items such as pens or magnets. With a little creative thinking, swag can be a constant, lasting reminder of the incubator.

To celebrate the opening of The New Century Venture Center in 1996, Ison threw an open house and issued invitations in the form of egg-shaped mouse pads featuring the incubator's chicken mascot. The mouse pads cost a little less than $2 each. "They were a big hit," she says. "I still see them around."

For the 2005 opening of the Thunderbird Global Incubator, Hisrich spent $680 on one hundred coffee cups, four hundred pens, and five hundred squeezable stress balls imprinted with the incubator's name and logo. He gave them away to students, faculty, and anyone attending when he spoke to a community group. The stress balls, especially, were popular. "Everybody's used to cups and pens, but nobody had stress balls," he says.

Promotional items are "the best bang for the advertising dollar there is," Hisrich says, because you control to their distribution. "When you are able to give these promos to people who are in your potential market or will see people in your potential market, you have far less waste exposure," he says. "And you have exposure for a longer period of time because the cup or the stress ball will be on their desk where lots of people will see it."

While a pen or coffee cup puts your brand in front of a single user every day, a T-shirt may be noticed by hundreds every time it's worn. Tony Antoniades, general manager of the Advanced Technology Development Center in Atlanta, Georgia, has T-shirts made every year featuring the names and logos of all incubator clients on the back and the ATDC logo on the front. "There's a lot of pride in wearing the shirts," he says. "[Clients say,] 'My company logo is on the back, and look at all the other company logos.' It gets some conversation going."

Those logos, however, can be the most difficult part of getting the shirts made. Every company has to provide a high-quality version of its logo, and getting those takes a lot of legwork, Antoniades says. Then he has to find a printer that can reproduce the logos faithfully. "If a blue logo turns purple, it ruins the whole logo," he says.

Each T-shirt costs about $10 to produce, Antoniades says, which includes design, printing, and shipping. He usually finds a sponsor to cover the cost and puts the sponsor's name on the shirt sleeve. For example, in 2006, the shirts were sponsored by HIG Ventures, an investment company. "They know that if they can get on the sleeve of those T-shirts, they can give them away to other investors," Antoniades says. "It's their way to say, 'We're involved in a lot of these companies and in supporting ATDC.'"

Each client gets a T-shirt. Others are given to ATDC staff, volunteers, and student interns, as well as to potential sponsors and partners. "Nobody turns down a T-shirt," Antoniades says. His goal for the shirts—other than promoting ATDC and its clients—is simple: "I want to get enough out there that I'll be at the grocery store and see somebody wearing one," he says.

Direct Mail

While advertising goes out to a mass audience in hopes of reaching a wide swath of a targeted market, direct mail is sent only to a very specific group or groups. It's less expensive than display or broadcast advertising, but can be costly nevertheless when you add up the cost of paper, envelopes, printing, postage, and possibly the purchase of a mailing list.

Direct mail may be most effective when it's used to reach not entrepreneurs, but those who encounter them often. Arizona's Hisrich did just that to promote the opening of the Thunderbird Global Incubator. He sent 300 personal letters to banks, CPAs, accounting firms, and others who service small businesses, using a mailing list he acquired (free of charge) from his local chamber of commerce. "I asked for their participation in getting the word out [and asked] what assistance they

Playing by the Direct Mail Rules

Under federal law, consumers have the right to opt out of direct mail solicitations, particularly those delivered by fax or e-mail.

Since April 2006, the Telephone Consumer Protection Act has required organizations to have an "established business relationship" with anyone to whom it sends an unsolicited fax promoting products, services, or property. Under Federal Communications Commission guidelines, a business relationship is established with anyone who uses or has used your services (such as current and former clients and those who have registered for seminars or workshops at your incubator), as well as anyone who inquires about your program or services. You also can collect fax numbers from ads, business cards, and Web sites unless those items specifically prohibit unsolicited faxes.

Under the CAN-SPAM Act of 2003, any e-mail that promotes or advertises a product or service has to clearly state the sender's name, e-mail address, originating domain name, and valid physical postal address; the subject of the message itself; and that the e-mail is intended as an advertisement or solicitation.

Both the TCPA and CAN-SPAM require senders to offer recipients a way to opt out of receiving future messages. The opt-out notice has to be noticeable (on the first page of faxes) and explain clearly how recipients can remove their fax number or e-mail from your mailing list. Fax opt-out mechanisms—whether by phone, fax, or online—must be free of charge and available around the clock, seven days a week. E-mail opt-outs must use a return e-mail address or other Web-based mechanism.

For information on fax advertising regulations, visit *www.fcc.gov/cgb/consumerfacts/unwantedfaxes.html*. An explanation of CAN-SPAM rules is available at *www.ftc.gov/bcp/conline/pubs/buspubs/canspam.htm*.

could provide to our companies," he says. The campaign netted Hisrich several partners, including a law firm and an accounting firm, each of which sends representatives to the incubator for a half-day weekly to give advice to Thunderbird clients.

E-mail provides an even less expensive option, especially if your mailing list is large. The Women's Technology Cluster in San Francisco, California, offers at least two workshops or seminars a week, plus a regular schedule of high-profile events such as conferences and symposiums. To promote those events, WTC e-mails some seven thousand people at least once a week.

"It's the most efficient way for us to do outreach for our events," says Megan Watkins, who was WTC's program and marketing associate from 2005 to 2006.

WTC amassed the seven thousand e-mails on its list largely through data capture—collecting the e-mail addresses of everyone who had attended a WTC event, for example. E-mails to WTC's two hundred mentors request that they copy WTC if they forward the message to someone else; the program then captures those e-mail addresses, too. For a few hundred dollars a year, WTC also subscribes to a Silicon Valley venture capital mailing list.

Preparing an e-mail to promote a new event, such as WTC's First Annual Angel Investor Colloquium in May 2006, may take a few hours. For regular events, such as WTC's biweekly legal seminars, each "blast" takes about twenty minutes to write and send.

"It would take me a lot more time to physically leave the office and distribute flyers," Watkins says. "Plus printing flyers can be quite expensive, and mailing gets expensive. It's much easier for us to do this via e-mail."

WTC subscribes to Topica, an online marketing service that maintains WTC's e-mail database and distributes the messages. Sending the message is as simple as copying and pasting, choosing a mailing list, and hitting "send." The service also can track who opened the e-mail and how many clicked through to WTC's Web site to register for a particular event.

"There are a number of online services, so it's getting less and less expensive to maintain lists and do blasts," Watkins says. "There are more and more ways to do online [direct] marketing for very little money or for free."

A good tip from Lesley Anne Rubenstein, chief executive of the Thames Innovation Centre in London, England: when using e-mail to promote an event, don't describe the event in full. Instead, give a teaser and provide a link to your Web site, or require users to register online. That drives traffic to your Web site, which not only lets users learn more about your program, but also boosts your site's profile on Google, which returns results based on site traffic.

Outreach

Many incubators promote their facilities and services by offering seminars and workshops, hosting events, and participating in trade shows. Such events raise an incubator's profile among targeted audiences and prime the pool of potential clients by improving entrepreneurs' skills and knowledge to make their businesses more likely to succeed.

Training programs. Seminars and workshops for clients and the community at large can serve myriad purposes: helping clients strengthen their businesses, attracting potential clients, raising awareness of the incubator's mission, and making the area's entrepreneurial pool deeper and broader. Topics can range from the basic (such as how to develop a business plan or maintain cash flow) to the very specific, like commercializing technology or applying for government grants.

The @Wales Digital Media Initiative

uses its monthly training events as a way to market programs and services to potential clients. Each event has a general topic, such as developing brand image or profiting from intellectual property, and is conducted as a two-hour workshop, with time for socializing and networking.

"The main way we get clients is through the marketing and networking events that we run," says Jones of @Wales. "The [events] will attract sometimes quite a significant number of people—over one hundred, which is a lot for that sort of event. It gets the word out about what we do and gets different companies talking to each other."

Sometimes, entrepreneurs sign on to become incubator clients soon after attending a training event. But more often, training is a long-term investment in growing a community's entrepreneurial pool. In fact,

Marketing Methods Overview

There are many different marketing vehicles you can use to reach your target markets. Some methods might be better for reaching a particular audience than others. Don't worry so much about how many different methods you use—it's better to use a few methods effectively than to use lots of different approaches haphazardly.

Advertising
- Television
- Newspaper
- Magazine
- Radio
- Web
- Permanent signage
- Temporary banners

Testimonials
- Satisfied clients and graduates
- Leaders of peer organizations
- Well-known community leaders

Promotional Items
- T-shirts
- Pens
- Stress balls
- Mouse pads
- Coffee cups
- Etc. – be as creative as you wish

Direct Mail
- Postcards
- Personalized letters
- Special offers
- E-mail

Outreach
- Seminars
- Workshops
- Training programs
- Industry conferences
- Trade shows

Events
- Anniversary celebrations
- Business plan competitions
- Venture or angel investment forums

Public Relations
- Press releases
- News conferences
- Letters to the editor
- Opinion-editorial pieces

Publications
- Brochures
- Newsletters
- Web sites
- Annual reports

Networking
- Speaking engagements with local civic and business groups
- Personal contacts with local business leaders
- Organizing opportunities for business and civic leaders to interact with incubator clients

some incubators specifically offer fundamental business training for nascent entrepreneurs who are not yet ready to become incubator clients. For example, the Central Valley Business Incubator conducts pre-incubation workshops that allow potential entrepreneurs to interact with other business owners and become comfortable with the incubator setting, easing their way into tenancy, says CVBI's Furtado, the incubator's former chief operating officer.

You don't have to come up with a training program from scratch. Many incubators offer courses from FastTrac, a product of the Ewing Marion Kauffman Foundation of Kansas City, Missouri, or NxLevel, developed by the University of Colorado Center for Community Development.

The Springfield Business Incubator in Springfield, Massachusetts, hosts a NxLevel course that has proven to be a pipeline for new clients. "Four of my current tenants have taken the class," says Director Deborah L. King. "They may have taken it three years ago, but at least they've been to the building, and getting them in the building is half the battle."

She chose a commercial class for its ease of administration. The incubator is a program of Springfield Technical Community College; its Center for Business and Technology, which offers continuing education classes, handles the NxLevel registrations. King works with the same accredited NxLevel instructor each time. "I just meet with her about when to offer the class and meet with our designer for promotional cards," she says. "It's not a tremendous amount of my time."

King usually lines up a sponsor to cover most of the cost of the class; as a result, she's able to charge $150 for the course instead of $400. The fee ensures that applicants will follow through on attendance and participation. "If we had the class fully sponsored it would be a disincentive for commitment," King says. "Now they get a good deal, but they're still invested." Sponsors usually are banks, which get to make a presentation during the course. "They can do a piece on financials, and get to meet fifteen people who are starting businesses," King says.

The ultimate in training outreach, however, may come from LBTC. The incubator already received funding from the Louisiana Department of Economic Development and the Greater Baton Rouge Chamber of Commerce to provide training and education to small businesses outside the incubator. Then, in 2004, the incubator received an unusual donation: an eighteen-wheel truck worth $300,000. With the help of a $135,000 grant from the U.S. Department of Agriculture, D'Agostino turned the truck into a mobile classroom and launched a new outreach program, "Driving Louisiana's Economy," to bring business training to rural communities throughout the state.

The mobile classroom is equipped with broadband wireless Internet connectivity and state-of-the-art audio and visual capabilities, and can seat up to thirty people. Programs offered include how to start and finance a small business, how to write a business plan, how to take a home-based business to the next level, and how technology companies can compete for SBIR grants.

The program will help LBTC expand its reach beyond the incubator's walls, D'Agostino says. "To have a major impact on Louisiana's economy, we felt we had to take entrepreneurship and business incubation on the road to reach as many people as possible, especially underserved entrepreneurs in rural Louisiana," he says.

The project also caught the attention of the media; the BBC, National Public Radio, and *The Wall Street Journal* all published stories about it. "You can't buy that type of publicity," D'Agostino says.

Events. If workshops and seminars are the meat and potatoes of incubator outreach, special events are dessert: something to indulge in occasionally, and certainly memorable when executed well.

As their program approached its twentieth anniversary, the staff of the Nashville Business Incubation Center in Nashville, Tennessee, wanted to do something to commemorate the occasion. They found their answer at the 2005 NBIA International Conference on Business Incubation, during a session on a long-running business plan competition in Philadelphia, Pennsylvania.

"I said, 'That's exactly what we need to do,'" says Mildred Walters, the incubator's executive director. "We didn't want to just have a chicken dinner and move on."

Walters and Angela Crane-Jones, the incubator's assistant director, spent nearly a year planning and running the competition. About half of the time was spent raising $125,000, including a total of $45,000 in prizes. "The competition paid for itself," Walters says. "We even made a little money."

The competition opened in October 2005 with announcements in local media. By early December, some three dozen applicants had paid a $100 entry fee. The commitment took more than just money; contestants were required to enroll in a ten-week FastTrac training course, which the incubator usually offers only to its clients. "Several people had come to us [in the past] and asked, 'Can't you do [training] for other people?'" she says.

The course also helped to narrow the field: by the time it was done, only twenty-five competitors remained. Those still standing submitted final business plans to a panel of judges, which selected ten finalists. The winner was revealed at a June 2006 gala with 250 people in attendance.

The winner of the competition received $25,000 in cash and prizes donated by area businesses, and a year's free residency at the incubator. Second and third place netted $10,000 and $5,000, respectively, in cash and prizes. A separate award—named for NBIC founding director Jennie W. Lemons, who stepped down in 2002 after eighteen years with the incubator—included $5,000 in cash and prizes.

Throughout the process, the incubator scored lots of publicity. "[The competition] captured the imagination of all the business writers in town," Walters says. "It was almost like a reality show—you start off with thirty people and end up with one."

After that first competition and gala, Walters and Crane-Jones took a six-month break before knocking on doors in February 2007 to raise funds for a second competition.

"We decided we'll do this every other year because it takes a year to [plan and implement]," Walters says.

Not every event has to be quite so elaborate; neither does it have to come from an operating incubator. In June 2006, New York's Adirondack Regional Business Incubator sponsored its first event—before it even had a facility. Dubbed "The Thinkubator," the event (held at the offices of the Adirondack Regional Chambers of Commerce in Glens Falls) offered entrepreneurs the opportunity to present their business ideas to a customized panel of local accountants, lawyers, marketers, and bankers, who provided feedback.

The event was intended not only to promote the incubator, but also to help its organizers get a better handle on their market. The incubator's feasibility study had looked at filings for business licenses and other traditional measures, "but we also were looking for those who hadn't filed an application yet or were working at home," says Executive Director Peter Wohl.

Wohl also wanted to make sure that the event (and, later, the incubator) reached entrepreneurs from every corner of Warren County. The southern end of the county

Keeping an Event Fresh and Relevant

The Lennox Tech Enterprise Center in Rochester, New York, offered its first Tech Entrepreneurs' Week in 1997 as a way to introduce the incubation program to the community. The plan succeeded: by the fourth TEW, Lennox was full, and the week's seminars and social events drew seventy to one hundred entrepreneurs each. TEW even won the 2002 NBIA Incubator Innovation Award.

But times changed, says Paul Wetenhall, president of High Tech Rochester, which sponsors Lennox. "We went from being the sole voice for entrepreneurial support [around Rochester] to being one of many voices," he says, pointing to the formation of an incubator at the Rochester Institute of Technology and growing entrepreneurial programs at the University of Rochester. And as Lennox became more well known, more clients were coming from referrals by graduates and partners, not through TEW. "Our need to use TEW as a key driver had declined because we had other sources of prospects," Wetenhall says.

To accommodate the changing environment, Lennox offered the first Rochester Entrepreneurship Conference in fall 2003, with a full day of speakers and breakout sessions. TEW made its final bow in 2004; in January 2006, the Rochester Entrepreneurship Conference returned under the combined aegis of HTR, RIT, the University of Rochester, and Greater Rochester Enterprise, the regional economic development organization. The 2006 event drew 180 attendees; future conference sites will alternate between the university and RIT.

Cooperation among the four institutions is necessary, Wetenhall says, because of the size of the conference: four sessions in each of three tracks (start-ups, growth, and technology) plus two keynote speakers. The $20,000 conference budget is covered primarily by sponsors, but the planning and promotion fall primarily to the university, RIT, and HTR.

"The conference cements a very tight relationship between HTR and the two leading institutions of higher education in town," Wetenhall says. And because both of those institutions are considerably larger than HTR—the university is the city's largest employer, and RIT has 15,000 students—participating in the conference planning and sponsorship is vital to Lennox's continued success. "It's a way of cementing in the community our leadership role relative to entrepreneurship," Wetenhall says.

Phasing out a proven and popular event can seem daunting, but Wetenhall says it's more important not to stagnate. "For us, it was about not becoming fixated on something we did and loved," he says. "It's easy sometimes to stick to the old way of doing things, but you have to adapt when it's appropriate."

---

is relatively urban, with the city of Glens Falls and surrounding suburbs. Most of the northern part of the county, however, lies on the edges of or within Adirondack Park, the largest publicly protected area in the contiguous United States, and thus is extremely rural. Wohl blanketed the county with an eye-catching poster, designed by a local firm, and made applications available in the newspaper, online, and by telephone.

In all, Wohl set up twelve panels for entrepreneurs with business ideas centered on everything from health-care administration to music downloads. To ensure each entrepreneur's comfort, Wohl tailored each panel not only to individual entrepreneurs' ideas, but also to their environment. "If [the entrepreneur] was from the northern part of the county, we made sure that panel had someone from the northern part of the county," Wohl says.

He deemed the event a success, both as a measure of the market and an advertising tool. "We got a sense that there are a lot of folks tinkering in basements who haven't taken the next steps to formalize their idea," Wohl says. "We hope to make this an annual event to add to the pipeline" of potential clients for the incubator.

Trade shows. Trade shows can be an effective means of reaching a particular audience. For example, many incubators and research parks exhibit at the annual BIO International Convention, the largest biotechnology conference in the world. (Incidentally, in the Angelou Economics survey cited at the beginning of this chapter, respondents ranked BIO as the top industry trade show.)

Vicki Jenings, director of business relations for the Fitzsimons Redevelopment Authority in Aurora, Colorado—which includes a bioscience incubator—has exhibited at BIO since 1999. "The real value is not to come home with a list of possible tenants, but to be able to let the rest of the world know that we have a bioscience agenda and infrastructure, that we're in the game," Jenings says.

Exposure also was the impetus for Aaron Miscenich's first trip to BIO in 2006, on behalf of the New Orleans BioInnovation Center in New Orleans, Louisiana, where he is executive director. "I thought it was important to get our name out there and let people know that New Orleans is open for business," he says.

Both Jenings and Miscenich included their exhibits in larger pavilions run by their states' economic development departments, a move that saved money (it's much less expensive than shipping and setting up a lone booth, they say) and made sure they weren't lost in the mass of more than one thousand exhibits. "There is strength in numbers, not just in the cost, but in notice," Jenings says. "A state pavilion is noticed more than a single booth. And you add to your state's message—having a bioscience incubator is a huge asset."

Being noticed was especially important for Miscenich, whose program is one of three bioscience incubators funded by the Louisiana Department of Economic Development. But while the other two programs (in Baton Rouge and Shreveport) had opened by 2006, Miscenich's hadn't; construction of his facility was delayed by Hurricane Katrina, and he knew he faced an uphill battle in promoting his program. "I was trying to overcome a lot of negative perceptions," he says. "There are people who are tired of hearing about New Orleans; there are those who [thought] we were still awash; and there are those who [thought] everything is back to normal." By participating in BIO, Miscenich says, he was able to show a positive side to the city's recovery, while emphasizing the need for business investment in the Crescent City.

Both Jenings and Miscenich went well supplied with brochures and newsletters. In addition, Jenings budgets about $6,000 for one full-page color ad in one of the following magazines: *Site Selection*, *Expansion Management*, or *Facilities*. That also nets her an article in the magazine she selects; all of them are distributed at BIO. "It may be the only time of the year that we do magazine advertising," she says.

BIO is a huge conference—the 2006 event had more than 1,700 exhibitors and almost twenty thousand attendees. Even at a smaller event, though, it can be hard to get noticed. The most successful exhibitors lure participants with more than brochures.

When Colorado redesigned its BIO pavilion, Jenings got to add her ideas. She also learned that the new pavilion would include plasma TV, so she splurged $15,000 on an eleven-minute video about Fitzsimons that ran continually throughout the conference. She's getting plenty of bang for the buck, screening the video during monthly tours of the Fitzsimons facilities and for prospective clients and tenants.

Miscenich, on the other hand, was much more low-tech, providing a taste of New Orleans—literally—by offering pralines made by a small New Orleans company. "They were a hit and went really fast," he says.

The expenses can add up—Jenings budgets up to $5,000 for her BIO booth each year, plus another $1,500 for travel and meals—but it's a good investment. Jenings says it's a way to show that her program is a player in Colorado's bioscience industry, not only to developers and companies, but also to legislators who often attend the show. For Miscenich, exposure to industry vendors and service providers was most valuable. "I'm looking to bring an established company into my building as a partner who can enhance the clientele and provide services to them and the community as well," he says.

You don't have to travel across the country and spend thousands to reap the benefits of a trade show. While the Louisiana Business & Technology Center also has a booth in the Louisiana Pavilion at BIO, director D'Agostino also always has a display at the Baton Rouge business expo. "We show off some of the tenants in the incubator, pass out materials, and talk to people about our workshops and training programs and possible space in the incubator," D'Agostino says.

The payoff benefits both the incubator and its clients, he says. "By participating in

Making the Most of a Trade Show Exhibit

Participating in a trade show requires a significant investment of your time, and possibly a hefty layout of cash, too, so it's not a project to undertake lightly. "Think about what you're trying to achieve," says Stephani Delisio, who as NBIA's director of development secures sponsors and exhibitors for NBIA events. "How does that show help you meet your goals? Compare that information with the benefits the trade show will give you as an exhibitor." For example, if you're hoping to connect with potential sponsors or partners, will you get a list of show registrants and their contact information?

Also think about logistics, Delisio says. It's not just the cost of the space; consider the number of people you'll need to keep the booth staffed properly, how you're going to get your items to the show, and all the things you'll need to create an eye-catching booth. If you determine that trade show participation is worth your while, here are some other tips from Delisio to maximize your experience.

- For the best flow of people past your booth, try to get a spot close to a food or drink station.
- Make your booth area inviting. Don't put a table at the front of your booth spot; keep that area open so you can be right up front to greet attendees.
- Choose outgoing, energetic people to staff your booth.
- Offer a demonstration of some kind. "Determine the best way to showcase your service in a short amount of time," Delisio says.
- Giveaways are nice, but make sure you're getting something in return. "Ask for a business card before they can take an item," Delisio says.
- "If you're going to the expense of exhibiting, take advantage of all the benefits offered by the trade show," Delisio says. If you get free tickets for receptions, show up ready to work the room. If you get a mailing list of participants, use it.
- When you get home, evaluate the experience. Did you get a good return on your investment? What could you have done differently?

Marketing Methods

events like [this], LBTC gets great exposure to potential incubator clients and resource service providers for our network," he says. "Lenders and investors have visited our booth to pick up information on our companies to contact them later for loans, investments, or to purchase products or services."

Public Relations

Public relations is the organized effort you make to present your incubation program in a positive way to clients, partners, sponsors, stakeholders, the media, and the community in general. Effective public relations help establish your incubation program's image and reputation, both of which are key to attracting new clients, partners, and sponsors, as well as shoring up community support.

Publicity and media relations. Publicity—unpaid communication in the media about the incubator—is one of the most effective ways to establish your incubation program's image and reputation. Consumers generally place more trust in a newspaper article or a spot on the evening news than in advertising because they perceive that a paid message is more likely to be biased; the advertiser, after all, is going to put only the good stuff in an ad.

LBTC's D'Agostino issues a press release about the incubator or its clients nearly every day, and as a result either his program or his clients appear in the local media every week. D'Agostino usually drafts the press releases himself or, if one of his interns from Louisiana State University (the incubator's sponsor) is a good writer, he has the student write it. The final draft goes to the university's public relations department, which formats the press release according to university style and sends it out. "We used to put out our own press releases, but that's not what I get paid to do," D'Agostino says. "Since university PR is willing to do that, we ship it out to them."

Incubation programs offer myriad stories and photo opportunities. That's the good news. The bad news is, your incubation program probably is not the only source of business news in your area. To get your share of news space, you may have to work a little harder than the competition to attract the media spotlight.

One of the first steps is to know who you're dealing with. Getting to know the reporters and editors who cover the news can mean the difference between a press release that leads to a story and a press release in a recycling bin.

"It's about establishing that personal relationship with the media," says Amoskeag's Gustafson. She makes regular calls to contacts such as the business editor of the *Manchester Union Leader*, New Hampshire's leading newspaper. "I'm on great terms with him," she says. "I often call him to let him know I'm sending a press release, and we chat."

The personal touch extends to the kinds of stories that pique editors' interest. Clients' stories often are the most compelling because they put a human face on business success, says Mark Lieberman, manager of regional and economic development with the Community Development Commission of Los Angeles County, which sponsors the Business Technology Center of Los Angeles County in Altadena, California. "Your clients are the real story," he says. "Their stories are so rich. If you tell a good story, great; if you're a part of that story, even better."

Here's an example of how that can work. In late 2005, Jan DeYoung, executive director of the St. Louis Enterprise Centers in St. Louis, Missouri, met with Ellen Sherberg, publisher of the *St. Louis Business Journal*, about sponsoring NBIA's 20th International Conference on Business Incubation, which was to take place in St. Louis the following spring. In passing, DeYoung mentioned that one of his incubation facilities was adding a shared-use

Tips for Better Publicity Photos

Photos are a quick and easy way to grab attention for your incubation program, especially when the media are involved. Editors are always on the lookout for something of visual interest to run in their publications, and given the choice between two stories of similar news value, they often will give priority to the one with a photo.

Getting great photos of your incubator doesn't necessarily mean hiring a professional photographer. If you're on a tight budget, you easily can do it yourself. Here are some tips to get you started.

- **Cover the basics.** We can't speak for all media professionals, but NBIA's publications department likes to see photos of incubator facility exteriors as well as everyday activities going on inside, such as clients baking bread at a kitchen incubator, using high-tech equipment at a biotech incubator, or assembling parts at a mixed-use incubator. We also frequently need photos of the incubator managers we interview. These are all basic shots you can use over and over again, not only to accompany news releases, but also in brochures, newsletters, and on your Web site.

- **Mark the occasion.** If you're too busy to take photos on an average workday, make a habit of snapping a few shots on special occasions, such as a grand opening, an incubator-sponsored workshop, or a client graduation ceremony. Coverage of these events will impress stakeholders, attract potential clients, and raise community awareness.

- **Strive for quality.** The images you capture of your incubator must display sharp focus and good light. Dark, blurry photos rarely will make it into a print publication.

- **Make the most of digital photos.** Increasingly, editors prefer digital images to actual prints. In general, print publications require images at least five inches by seven inches in size that are saved in JPEG or TIFF format at a high resolution (at least three hundred dots per inch or dpi.). Don't expect reporters or editors to "grab" photos from your Web site. Photos on the Web are displayed at a lower resolution (seventy-two dpi) than is needed for print publication.

- **Get caption information.** A published photo usually requires a caption, so be sure to provide the first and last names of any people in the photo (from left to right) and where and when the photo was taken. When applicable, provide the photographer's name for a photo credit.

kitchen and that he already had clients for it, including DB Gourmet Cookies, a company founded by three friends who first baked cookies to raise money for college. Although established in telecommunications careers, they re-formed the business not only to sell cookies, but also to offer entrepreneurship experiences to children, who help with sales and production.

"Ellen said, 'Oh, we've got to write about them sometime,'" DeYoung says. "Bam, the next day we had a call from a reporter." Shortly thereafter, the newspaper published a lengthy story about the incubator and DB Gourmet Cookies, along with a color photograph of the company's founders. Other media outlets picked up the story, including *Sauce*, a magazine devoted to regional restaurants and cuisine.

"The phone just started ringing off the hook and we started getting referrals," DeYoung says. "Once people heard about the kitchen, we got tons of calls." The same thing happened after the *St. Louis Post-Dispatch* ran an article on DB Gourmet Cookies in November 2006, DeYoung says.

Another good way to turn clients' successes into incubator publicity is to nominate them for awards. When Glenn Doell was director of the Rensselaer Incubator Program in Troy, New York, he made a point of nominating clients for any award he could find. As a result, Rensselaer clients were named start-up company of the year by the local business journal for three years straight. Another was selected as NBIA's 1995 Outstanding Incubator Client. (Rensselaer was named Randall M. Whaley Incubator of the Year then as well.)

"When clients won such awards, they'd get lots of local press—we'd make sure of that with our own press releases and newsletters," says Doell, now director of technology transfer at Greene, Tweed & Co. in Kulpsville, Pennsylvania. The media attention helped to enhance the incubator's reputation as well. "Potential clients would naturally want to be associated with award-winning clients and an award-winning incubator," Doell says.

You don't have to wait for a client or graduate to win an award, though. "Sometimes, you have to help them make the news," D'Agostino says. As part of his aggressive public relations efforts, D'Agostino constantly reminds his clients and graduates about the importance of sharing their successes through the media. As a result, those success stories appear frequently in news reports throughout the state—almost always with positive mention of LBTC.

To learn more about how to write and distribute press releases, as well as other vehicles for media relations, see Appendix A.

Publications

Publications include brochures, newsletters, Web sites, and reports—anything you publish (in print or electronically) to communicate about your incubator.

Brochures. Many incubators' first publication is a brochure, which can be distributed to potential partners, sponsors, clients, and other stakeholders. There are lots of brochures out there, so yours has to deliver its information in a compelling way that stands out.

One way to do that is to think beyond the traditional trifold format. Prospective clients and partners of the Advanced Technology Development Center get a customized packet of materials in pre-printed folders. Antoniades ordered one thousand folders printed in ATDC's colors on a heavy, smooth, matte stock, and fills them with information targeted to the recipient. For example, potential investors receive a list of ATDC clients and a separate sheet with current data on investments and investors in ATDC clients, as well as mergers and acquisitions. For potential clients, he includes a similar one-sheet brochure on ATDC itself that explains what the program is and what it does. (When ATDC moved into a new facility, Antoniades ordered stickers with the incubator's new address and applied them over the old address on the folders.)

Another approach comes from the Northern Alberta Business Incubator in St. Albert, Alberta, Canada, which publishes an annual program guide. The eight-page booklet includes descriptions of and dates for workshops and seminars, as well as general information about the incubation program and its staff.

"The theme goes from introductory stuff for people who aren't sure if they want to be in business for themselves all the way through personal coaching for entrepreneurs," says Managing Director Dar Schwanbeck.

While their approaches are different, both employ similar strategies to curb costs. Both Antoniades and Schwanbeck use high-quality color laser printers to print PDF files of their brochures. While Schwanbeck will print one hundred or two hundred copies of his brochure at a time, Antoniades runs off the individual information sheets as needed.

"We can print them on demand so we don't have five hundred of them lying around," Antoniades says. While the per-piece cost is higher than Antoniades would pay for pre-printed brochures, the overall cost is much lower—only good paper and color laser toner—and he gains immediacy. "I'll call our graphic design firm and say, 'Change this' or 'Change that,'" Antoniades says. "They send me a new PDF and we're done." (Another advantage with PDFs: they're easily posted for downloading from your Web site.)

Whether you print them yourself or have them run at a traditional printer, brochures are the place to splurge on design. Antoniades works with the same graphic design firm for all his materials. "We want to look professional and see a common theme in everything," he says. Because the firm does so much work for ATDC—and because Antoniades has introduced the firm to so many clients, including departments at the Georgia Institute of Technology, ATDC's sponsor—the company usually charges nothing for small changes to brochures and other quick-turnaround jobs. "They do stuff for us without nickel and diming us," Antoniades says.

Schwanbeck spends about $1,500 for design of his program booklet, then has it updated once during the year. A slightly smaller, two-color version of the brochure is inserted into the local newspaper twice a year. "It's an unbelievable deal," he says. "I got eight full pages of advertising for $1,100."

As with design, it's worth the investment to hire a professional photographer. You can use the photos in your brochure, your press kit, on your Web site, and anytime you need a powerful, high-quality picture to represent your program. Many professional photographers now use digital cameras, so you can keep all the pictures from a particular shoot

> ## Great Guides for Design and Writing
>
> Most incubator managers are not professional designers or copywriters. You can, however, improve your eye for design and your ear for good writing with the help of some classic guides.
>
> - *The Non-Designer's Design Book* by Robin Williams (Peachpit Press, 2003). The title says it all. The author presents the basics of good design and typography in a simple way that will help anyone understand how to improve his or her publications.
> - *The Non-Designer's Web Book* by Robin Williams (Peachpit Press, 2000). While some design principles are universal, others are unique to the Web. This guide offers the same straightforward yet lighthearted approach to the Internet as Williams' book on print design.
> - *On Writing Well* by William K. Zinsser (Collins, 2006). This book is required reading for most introductory journalism classes, and for good reason: it's the bible of clear, simple writing.
> - *The Associated Press Stylebook* (Basic Books, revised 2006). Spelling, punctuation, capitalization, hyphenation—it's all in this handbook. You'll never mix up continuous and continual again, and your writing will be the better for it.
> - *The Elements of Style* by William Strunk Jr. and E.B. White (Longman, 2000). There are a plethora of grammar and punctuation guides out there, but this is the granddaddy of them all. It's small (105 pages) but packed with easy-to-understand guidance.

on a CD-ROM in your office, instead of having to get prints from the photographer when you need them.

If you're using traditional brochures, distribute them as widely as possible. Good places to stock your brochure include the offices of community organizations and

Marketing Methods

government entities that have an interest in your program, such as libraries, government licensing offices, chambers of commerce, banks, offices of economic development, venture fund offices, and area colleges and universities. Check back periodically to see if they need more. "If you really want to keep them there, you have to check in yourself," says New Hampshire's Gustafson.

Better yet is to make a brochure your second point of contact, Schwanbeck says. "Brochures are a wonderful follow-up piece, but you have to have some kind of initial contact," he says.

Newsletters. Newsletters enable you to maintain a valuable dialogue with your clients and community stakeholders. The best newsletters are filled with short, easily digested stories that offer a quick read. But don't let that fool you; publishing a good newsletter takes time and discipline.

"When we started with our first issue, we tried to write it ourselves," says Georgia's Antoniades. "We realized it was just too overwhelming." Now, the quarterly ATDC newsletter is written by a freelance writer, under the editorial supervision of a staff member who also does publications for Georgia Tech.

That costs Antoniades about $10,000 a year, but the newsletter has no other expenses related to it because it is solely electronic: each issue is distributed to its three thousand readers (including sponsors, partners, service providers, graduates, and representatives of Atlanta's many corporate headquarters) only by e-mail.

"One factor was cost," Antoniades says. "Another was that we didn't have mailing addresses for our contacts because we stopped collecting physical addresses from people years ago. We're a tech incubator, so all of our contacts use e-mail."

ATDC uses an online service to maintain its e-mail database and send the newsletter. The freelance writer formats the newsletter in a predesigned HTML template; Antoniades cleans up the layout as needed and adds pictures, then tests the e-mail before sending it to the list and posting the newsletter on the ATDC Web site. It takes about four hours each issue, he says, which may get shorter. "I want to use some of my grad students more for the testing," he says. "A lot of it is just clicking on links to make sure they work."

He started the newsletter in the summer of 2004. "I was posting news on our Web site, but unless readers went there, they wouldn't know about it," he says. "Investors want to know when we have new companies, and they don't want to wait for an open house or read about them in the newspaper."

The newsletter is a great vehicle for spreading the ATDC story and staying connected to stakeholders, he says. "The goal was to promote ATDC and brag about what we're doing here," he says. "One thing I didn't imagine was how it would open a dialogue. When it goes out, the reply-to address comes to me, and people I haven't talked to for a while will respond, 'Hey, I'm coming down next month, can I talk to this company?'"

Many readers still prefer a hard-copy newsletter. King, director of the Springfield Business Incubator, sends her *SBI Concepts* newsletter to some five hundred accountants, bankers, real estate agents, attorneys, and the like. "These people get so many e-mails, they may not even read mine," she says. "But I'm getting feedback [from the print version], so I know they're reading it."

She launched her newsletter in 2006 at the urging of a client who is "a whiz at sales and marketing," King says. After choosing her intended recipients for their potential to make referrals, King turned to another client whose company does photography and graphic design. King had collected newsletters from a variety of businesses and went over them with her designer. With a basic idea of what she wanted, King and the designer then worked with representatives of Springfield Technical Community College, which sponsors the incubator, to ensure that the final template would be consistent with the college's graphic identity standards.

King also put a good deal of thought into the content to keep a consistent message and to simplify production. Each issue includes lists of clients, supporting organizations, advisory board members, and upcoming events; a feature on a different client; and a guest column by a member of her advisory board. For example, the summer 2006 issue included an "intellectual property checklist" from an intellectual property attorney.

"They love that," she says of the opportunity for advisory board members to submit columns. "It promotes their business and they feel more involved with the incubator."

For each issue, King works with a freelance writer to come up with a list of stories to include. The writer handles all interviews, writing, and editing; King's only task is to review the final copy before it goes to the designer. "I couldn't possibly spend the time putting this together," she says.

In all, she spends about $1,800 for writing, design, printing of one thousand copies, and postage to mail five hundred issues. The remaining copies are distributed to the local chamber of commerce, the regional technology corporation, and "anywhere small businesses might go," King says.

"It's been great," she says of the response to the newsletter. "I've had people say, 'Gee, I saw your list of advisors. I'd like to

Tips for Optimum DIY Design

Sure, you'd love to have everything that comes out of your incubator benefit from the touch of a professional graphic designer. But that isn't always possible. Sometimes, whether for reasons of cost or time, you have to put something together yourself. For those times, here are some tips to make your amateur designs look more professional.

- **Limit the number of fonts.** A bunch of typefaces may seem like a way to jazz up a newsletter. In reality, lots of fonts are confusing and visually distracting. In general, choose one font for headlines and another for body text, and stick with them.
- **Think outside the box.** Avoid the temptation to draw frames or boxes around everything. It makes your layout look cluttered and interrupts the visual flow. Save the boxes for things you really want to emphasize.
- **Think like a typesetter.** If you're creating a flyer or newsletter in a word processing program, set the preferences to use curly quotes and apostrophes, long dashes, and other typographic punctuation.
- **Be judicious with clip art.** A little illustration goes a long way. Using too many images distracts from your message.
- **Stick together.** Keep subheadings with their text (not at the bottom of a column on their own) and place captions close to the pictures they describe.
- **Proofread.** This goes for everything you publish (and letters and memos), whether you do it yourself or hire a pro. Nothing says "amateur" faster than misspelled words, incorrect grammar, and poor punctuation.

be on your advisory board.' It's been really incredible."

Web sites. Increasingly, Web sites are the public's primary source of information about just about anything. An attractive, regularly updated Web site is an inexpensive way to get information about your incubator in front of potential clients and the public.

Above all, an incubator's Web site should reflect its mission and values—not only in content, but also in appearance. "Never forget that, more often than not, a Web site is the first impression of your organization," says Rubenstein of the Thames Innovation Centre. "If your Web site doesn't look professional, they're not going to contact you because they're going to figure that you're equally unprofessional." So it's vital to have a good-looking site that's easy to use, absolutely current, and free of misspellings and other errors.

As you would with any publication, you should start by considering what it is you want to communicate, and to whom. When she was director of the Canterbury Enterprise Hub in Canterbury, England, Rubenstein took a two-pronged approach to site content. "First is, what do clients want to know?" she says. "And because the Web site is a tool that helps me bring in deal flow, I ask, 'What will prospects be looking for?'"

As a result, the CEH Web site includes an extensive section on services—not just a single-page listing, but a complete menu with a page devoted to each service, explained in detail. A members-only section gives clients a way to update their contact and address information, set preferences for information from CEH, and participate in online forums.

Another section is devoted to news items submitted by sponsors. For example, in August 2006 the site featured a guide to common start-up mistakes from Business Link Kent, a clearinghouse for business-support and economic development services, as well as advice on patent specifications for manufacturers, provided by a legal firm that specializes in patent and trademark cases.

"The Sponsors News section is a way to add value for our sponsors," Rubenstein says. The sponsors provide the articles, but only the first paragraph or so appears on the CEH site. "You have to click the link to their site to read the rest—that's a payback to our sponsors," she says.

The site was designed and maintained by a CEH client. The incubator pays an annual fee of £1,500 (or about US $2,900) to the client that covers routine site maintenance; overhauls of the site, such as one undertaken in late summer 2006, incur an additional fee. Incubator staff can add events and other site content via a graphical interface, allowing them to keep the site fresh without waiting for help or needing to know HTML.

The interface was part of the initial design contract for the site, a requirement Rubenstein says every incubator manager should put in place. "It's crucial to anyone who has a Web site," she says. "If you have to keep going back to the people who [maintain] the site, you're wasting a lot of time." The site also was set up to automatically remove events after they occur, preventing the site from looking dated.

"You want everything that can be automated to be automated," she says. "You want it to work for you. We're all understaffed and under-budgeted, so any time you can save, you want to save."

A Web site can even become a revenue stream. The Houston Technology Center in Houston, Texas, prides itself on being "the center of technology entrepreneurship in Houston," as it proclaims on its home page.

"We were looking for creative ways to generate funds," says Hilla Barzilai-Abileah, the incubator's director of marketing and communications. "One of our strengths is our huge database. We have a very large database relative to our geographic concentration [of technology entrepreneurs]."

To maximize its outreach to potential clients for the least amount of money, HTC has made its Web site into a hub for information about the Houston technology scene and opportunities for start-ups. And the site gives users reasons to visit often, with an extensive calendar of events, white papers on various technology topics, and applications for its seed fund and incubator admission, among other features. "We get 160,000 page views per month," Barzilai-Abileah says.

Those numbers caught the eye of one of the incubator's advisors, who works with online advertising. "He said we have enough 'stickiness' here for people to want to use our site as another way to be involved with us," says former HTC President & CEO Paul M. Frison. So in mid-2006, HTC began selling advertising space on its home page.

What to Put on Your Web Site

At the minimum, your Web site should include:
- Your incubator's history and mission statement
- High-quality photographs of your facility, both inside and out
- A list of sponsors and partners
- Compelling information about your program's economic impact, such as the number of jobs created, wages paid to employees, etc.
- A list of your board of directors and/or advisors
- A list of client companies with links to their sites
- A schedule of upcoming events
- Complete contact information for the incubator, including names and titles of primary staff members, phone and fax numbers, e-mail addresses, and the incubator's physical and mailing addresses

To make the most of your site, consider including:
- Incubator press releases
- Case studies about successful clients or graduates
- Your newsletter and/or brochure in downloadable format
- Links to news articles about your incubator, clients, and graduates
- A video tour of your incubator facility
- Guidelines for application, including tips on preparing a business plan and the actual forms potential clients must complete and submit
- Links to relevant resources on business incorporation, business planning, funding sources, regulatory agencies, etc.

Another possible use of a Web site is to create a clients-only section accessible with assigned logins and passwords. A clients-only section of your site could include:
- Specific incubator policies and procedures
- An internal directory with names and contact information for all client companies
- Copies of your incubator logo for clients to include in their own marketing materials
- Contact information for partners who offer low- or no-cost services to incubator clients
- Business planning templates, tips, or software
- Forums where clients can exchange information and share ideas

It had immediate takers in FedEx Kinko's, Southwest Airlines, and Amegy Bank, which post ads at the side of each page of the site. Ad rates are based on the number of clicks the ads generate every month; the more times viewers click on a business' ad, the more that advertiser pays. While the program is young, Frison has high hopes for it. "We hope it will expand," he says.

Reports. An annual report doesn't have to be expensive. Many incubators compile data on their clients' and graduates' economic impact—such as number of employees, revenues, taxes paid, and so on—and publish it as a single-sheet brochure, in their newsletters, or on their Web sites. Some submit their numbers to a county or state economic development agency, which includes the information in its own annual report.

At the other end of the spectrum, however, is the glossy, four-color magazine-style report. Hobbs, general manager of the Toronto Business Development Centre, budgets $8,000 (Canadian) for his annual stakeholders' report, with eight pages of text and full-color photographs and artwork.

He published the first report in 2003, after TBDC received NBIA's Incubator of the Year award. "After we won the NBIA award, we said, 'We have to let everyone know what we're doing here,'" Hobbs says. "It's a way to educate our stakeholders as to what we're about and keep in their face."

While the first issue was more of an overview of TBDC, subsequent reports have established a more client-focused format. After an initial message from Hobbs (ghostwritten by the same freelance writer who prepares the rest of the copy), the report is split into sections that highlight the incubator's various programs by telling the stories of clients and graduates who have benefited from them.

"We want to tell [readers] what's going on now and tie in some grads to show what's happened before," Hobbs says. "More and more it's become about the clients, because people sell."

Throughout the year, Hobbs collects news reports and other information about clients and graduates. The staff then sits down to decide which stories will be the most compelling for the report. "It's a process of elimination because we always have more than we need," he says.

TBDC gives basic background information on the clients and graduates to be featured to a freelance writer, who does all the interviewing and writing. "There's only so much we can do," Hobbs says. "[The writer] adds the sizzle." A professional graphic designer handles the layout, providing several possible cover treatments to choose from. Some design elements on the cover and inside remain the same; for example, each cover has the TBDC logo at the top and the tagline "Toronto's Business Incubator: Empowering Toronto's Entrepreneurs" at the bottom.

While the actual writing and production process takes only a couple of months, Hobbs says the report really is a year-round project. "After we do one book, we start on the next," he says, starting the process of gathering information anew.

Hobbs prints three thousand copies of each report in December to avoid the busy summer vacation season and to coincide with the end of TBDC's fiscal year. About five hundred of them are mailed to government officials from the national to city levels, as well as to economic development agencies, industry groups, and business leaders. (He gets a break on postage costs because mailings to members of the national government are free.) The remainder serve as TBDC's brochure. "By the end of the year, we're out of them because we use them as marketing documents," he says.

The client-centered approach and the publication's professional look are worth the investment of time and money. "I've had letters back from the office of the premier of Ontario congratulating us on our fine work," Hobbs says. "And people will say, 'Oh, I know you guys, I saw your report.'"

Networking

Just because it's a cliché doesn't mean it's not true: it's not necessarily *what* you know, but *who* you know. "I've always had the philosophy that if we're going to open doors for clients, we have got to be plugged into the community," says LBTC's D'Agostino. "We pride ourselves in knowing the bank presidents, attorneys, and accountants. We get tremendous number of referrals from them."

Networking can be especially helpful to a new or developing incubator. In the months before the Innovation Center @ Wilkes-Barre opened in that Pennsylvania city in May 2004, John L. Augustine III appeared on radio and TV shows and spoke to civic and business groups about the incubator and its mission. "When you talk to a roomful of people, there may be fifteen of them who are thinking about starting a business," says Augustine, senior director of economic and entrepreneurial development with the Greater Wilkes-Barre Chamber of Business and Industry, which operates the incubator. The incubator's goal was to reach 35 percent occupancy by the end of its first year of operations. It hit that mark within five months and by its first birthday was nearly full—which Augustine credits, in part, to all those speaking engagements.

Personal appearances of that kind are important in an incubator's early days, says Thunderbird's Hisrich. "The center director or manager really needs to be a prime mover in the community," he says. Just as a new business is often closely identified, at first, with its founder, so is a new incubator personified by its leader. "In that case, the director *is* the incubator, so he or she needs to be out there a lot," he says.

Introducing incubation is only part of the networking equation. "Networking is about teaching and giving," says Lynne Waymon,

Reporting to the Community

Report reprinted with permission of the Toronto Business Development Centre

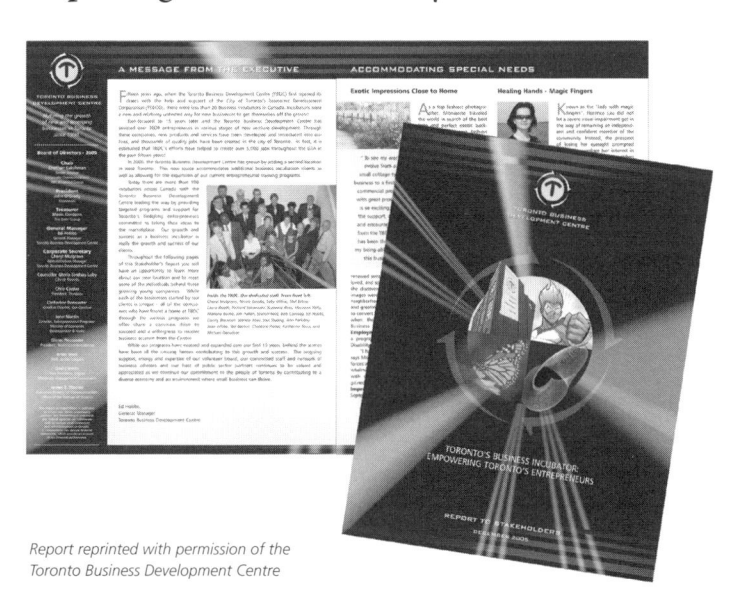

Every year, the Toronto Business Development Centre in Toronto, Ontario, Canada, produces a full-color, eight-page report about the incubator. Each incubator program or service is highlighted through the example of a client or graduate who has been successful because of TBDC. About five hundred are mailed to legislators, government officials, economic development agencies, industry groups, and business leaders. The remaining 2,500 serve as TBDC's brochure for that year.

author of *Make Your Contacts Count* (AMACOM, 2007) and president of Contacts Count, a networking consulting firm in Silver Spring, Maryland. "You're teaching people [about yourself], but also listening and trying to supply things that would be useful for them."

Los Angeles' Lieberman puts it another way. "Networking is a two-way street," he says. "It's about mutual satisfaction."

For example, Lieberman spends much of his time contacting attorneys, CPAs, marketing consultants, and others who serve entrepreneurs and inviting them to serve as mentors to his clients. He offers them an attractive quid pro quo: while providing their professional services free of charge, they get first crack at establishing business relationships with some of the region's up-and-coming technology companies.

When she led the Canterbury Enterprise Hub, Rubenstein played matchmaker between clients and service providers by initiating the "schmooze network," a regular series of evening get-togethers with drinks and snacks. "At first, it was just buying clients a drink at the pub," she says, "but not that many people turned up, so we decided to have a [speaker] and make it a little more formal."

Each gathering brings together Hub clients and board members, area business service providers, and students, faculty, and staff from the University of Kent, which sponsors the incubator, at a location on campus. Registration is required—and limited. Using information collected during registration, the staff creates a list of attendees for each event with contact and business information; the list is provided to everyone at the event. "You can mark who you want to talk to afterward," Rubenstein says. To help break the ice, "We purposely introduce people to each other so the right people are in touch with the right people," she says.

The broad mix of attendees (lubricated with a little wine) makes networking profitable for all, she says. Guests often linger after Hub staff leave, and many Hub clients have struck deals with investors or service providers they met through the network.

Introducing clients to funders or professionals can be as simple as opening your doors. Lieberman allows Southern California investment and entrepreneurial groups to use the center's conference rooms for meetings and other events. "If [a group] offers a service that is of use to my clients, I'm happy to host them," Lieberman says.

For example, the Pasadena Angels, a nonprofit group of investors who provide free business and financial planning advice to start-ups, holds its screenings in the center. Each month, the Angels hear presentations from up to six companies that would like the group to invest in them. BTCLAC clients are invited to attend to see how an investment presentation works.

"They get to see the presentations—the good, the bad, and the ugly," Lieberman says. Even better, clients can stay to hear the Angels' discussion of the presentations, in which they choose one or two companies to consider funding. "That is a true learning experience and invaluable as our clients prepare for their first round of funding," Lieberman says.

The arrangement with the Pasadena Angels worked so well that in 2005, the group became an anchor tenant in the incubator. "We want money people walking the hallways," Lieberman says. In addition to having potential investors right next door, BTCLAC clients also benefit from mentoring by Angels members, offered free of charge (complementing mentoring services provided by the incubator). Not to mention that "all 110 members of the Pasadena Angels are our ambassadors to the world, extolling our virtues," Lieberman says. "Imagine that—110 free salespersons!"

Sometimes, though, networking is just about good public relations. At LBTC, staff members are encouraged to participate actively in community groups such as the Red Cross, American Heart Association, or hospice. "If there's a meeting during working hours, they don't have to take vacation because they're presenting our image" as a

---

Three Key Moments in Networking

Networking is all about teaching and giving, says Lynne Waymon, author of *Make Your Contacts Count* (AMACOM, 2007) and president of Contacts Count, a networking consulting firm in Silver Spring, Maryland. You teach your contacts who you are and what you can do; you give them opportunities to succeed or move forward. That relationship begins with three key moments, and "great connectors know how to manage those moments," she says.

Before heading to a party, luncheon, or reception, think about what you will say during these three key moments. "You have to be prepared to be spontaneous," Waymon says.

The name exchange. When introducing yourself to someone new, help them to remember your name. "It's not their job to remember your name; it's your job to teach them your name," Waymon says. For example, I might say, "Hi, I'm Corinne Colbert. It's spelled French but pronounced American."

When the contact gives you his or her name, repeat it: "Hi, Ted, it's nice to meet you" or "Ted, let me take your coat." If it's an unusual name, ask the person to spell it and explain its origin. Another tip for remembering names is to find a personal connection—for example, "That's my son's name."

What do you do? "Most people miss the boat because they give the name of an organization or a job title, and neither of those cuts the mustard," Waymon says. She recommends the "best test answer": your best talent or skill and how that talent or skill has been tested. So instead of saying, "I'm director of the Peoria Business Incubator," you might say, "I put together government and community resources to help entrepreneurs succeed. One of my clients just got a $250,000 contract with one of our town's major hotels."

The trick, Waymon says, is to match your answer to the person you're talking to. The example above would be a good one to use with a potential client because it shows what you can do for them. A prospective partner, on the other hand, might be more impressed by your client or graduate roster: "We have thirty-three high-tech companies in our program and ten graduates that made $30 million in sales last year."

"This approach helps people see you in action," Waymon says. "It's so specific that they can't forget it, so it makes it easier for them to remember you."

How are you? This can be a conversation killer. "Usually the conversation is, 'How are you?' and you say, 'Not bad,' or 'What's new?' and you reply, 'Not much,'" Waymon says. To keep the conversation going, have a good answer ready. For example, when the contact asks, "How are you?" you could say, "I'm really excited—we just got word that we've been approved for a grant to expand our incubator."

It doesn't have to be something business related, either. "You're a human being, not just a job title, so it's fine to talk about leisure-time activities, especially when they show your character or your competence," Waymon says. So maybe the answer to "What's new?" is, "I coach my daughter's soccer team, and we're playing in the city championship this weekend."

Just be careful not to monopolize the conversation. Remember, your goal is not only to make yourself memorable, but also to learn about the other person. Ask them what they've been doing lately—"They can say they built a brick patio if they don't want to talk about work," Waymon says — or how they got interested in their career or hobby. Another tip: "Ask things like, 'If wanted to learn more about do-it-yourself bricklaying, how would I go about that?'" Waymon says. "People like to teach other people how to do things."

For more networking tips from Waymon, visit *www.contactscount.com*.

strong supporter of the region's overall well being, D'Agostino says.

Even a small gesture can go a long way. When Wayne Barz managed the Bridgeworks Enterprise Center in Allentown, Pennsylvania, one of his clients ran a chain of coffeehouses that served fresh-roasted coffee and pastries. To show his appreciation for referrals from area businesses and organizations, Barz would buy a tray of pastries and several carafes of coffee and have them delivered to the organization—"usually scheduled for whenever they were having a staff meeting," says Barz, now manager of entrepreneurial services for Ben Franklin Technology Partners of Northeast Pennsylvania in Bethlehem, Pennsylvania. "It was a great way to build goodwill and continued awareness."

If you don't happen to have a coffee-roaster or a baker among your clientele, you can use the same trick, he says. "Find someone locally that makes gift baskets or something like that," Barz says. "Be sure to include something with your incubator's brand on it as well. We used to have postcards with the incubator logo and contact information that we'd place around the goodies so you couldn't miss them. And if geography allows, deliver it yourself. You never know who you might get to tell your story to when you deliver something like that."

Conclusion

Whenever we here at NBIA set out to write a book about the incubation industry, we find ourselves in a quandary. The industry is as diverse as the entrepreneurs it serves. What applies to a mixed-use incubator in rural Oklahoma might not work at a biotechnology incubator sponsored by a major research university in a metro area, nor help a program focused on women in Eastern Europe.

But that variety is also what makes business incubation such a powerful economic engine. Every community has unique needs, its own history … its own market. All around the world, you can find successful business incubation programs founded on firm market research and run according to NBIA's principles and best practices.

So while our publications illustrate points with examples from established incubation programs, we don't mean to imply that those examples are the only way to go. They're just there to show you how one program has faced its challenges; how you apply those ideas to your situation is up to you.

With that in mind, here are some of the "big picture" ideas we hope you take away from this book.

- **Knowledge is power.** The more you know about your market, the better you can allocate your marketing resources. Whether you take on a major market survey or just ask around, what you learn may surprise you—and is sure to help you make more informed decisions.
- **Think about it.** A marketing plan, whether it's two pages or twenty, is a good investment of your time. It will give you a list of goals you hope to accomplish and a checklist of activities to accomplish them, as well as a way to measure whether what you're doing is working.
- **Make good use of partners.** Invite a marketing specialist, graphic designer, or commercial printer to join your board. They'll bring a unique perspective to incubator operations, and chances are you'll get inexpensive or free work as a result.
- **Don't be afraid to ask for a discount.** Many of those interviewed for this book got reduced prices on market research studies, graphic design, public relations, and

other expensive marketing activities just by asking for them.

- **Make marketing a learning experience.** Get help with marketing tasks by taking on student interns from a nearby college or university, or even a high school.
- **Look in your own backyard.** Who better to promote incubation than someone who's benefiting from it? If your clients or graduates include a designer or a public relations company, give them your business. If you don't have those resources in-house, look for home-based businesses. Many talented people are hiding out there, and they would relish the chance to show their stuff through such a high-profile client. (And who knows? Maybe they'll decide they're ready to get out of the house.)
- **Be creative.** Entrepreneurs want to be associated with other dynamic people and organizations. Stakeholders want to point to their association with the incubator with pride. So make sure your marketing presents your program as the dynamic, exciting, things-are-happening place it is.
- **Steal from the best.** Designers, writers, and similarly creative folks don't just pull their ideas out of thin air. They're always looking at what other designers, writers, and creative folks are doing and thinking about how they can apply those techniques to their latest project. So take a look at the materials on the CD-ROM that accompanies this book—and get your creative juices flowing.

APPENDIX A
Media Relations

Note: This guide to media relations was first published by NBIA in 2001 as a stand-alone toolkit called Get the Word Out! *It has been updated and is included here in its entirety.*

Does the word "media" conjure up an image of a rabid pack of news-hungry hounds on your doorstep? If so, it's time to change the way you view the press. Reporters operate in a mutually beneficial and mutually dependent relationship with the public and the business community. News professionals need your help identifying local stories to fill their publications and broadcasts. You need the media to help spread your message to potential clients, supporters, and the community.

Your goal in building relationships with media representatives is not to generate one-time news coverage; it is to set the stage for ongoing, professional coverage of your incubation program. Consider the time you spend introducing yourself to reporters and editors an investment in your program and your clients. The free publicity generated by news articles and other media coverage will increase the visibility of your organization.

Many of the basic rules of working with the media apply universally (e.g., give reporters information they can use, respect their deadlines, be available when they need you). However, the specific needs of media outlets vary widely. The best way to secure positive media coverage for your program is to understand the particular requirements of reporters in your area and to supply them with the information they need in a format they can use.

What is News?

News is, by definition, new information that describes recent or upcoming events or activities. Before contacting the press, determine if your message meets the following criteria. Does your news:

- Solve a problem?
- Offer something that will improve people's lives?
- Provide new information?

News Worth Reporting

Providing news tips to your local media outlets is one of the best ways to receive free publicity for your incubation program and your clients. However, flooding the media with inappropriate pitches may cause reporters to disregard your messages. News that is appropriate for one media outlet may be of no interest to another. For example, some print publications routinely cover job appointments, but radio and television stations rarely cover personnel moves (unless the person is a well-known figure in a high-level position).

The key to an effective media relations campaign is to understand both the definition of news and the particular coverage areas of the news organizations you are targeting. Some examples of newsworthy events your local media might be interested in covering are:

- Opening a new incubation program or facility
- Adding services to your incubation program
- Acquiring a new client
- Graduating a client
- Forming partnerships with other businesses or organizations
- Updating or adding to your facilities
- Receiving funding, both renewed and new
- Sponsoring a visit from a notable person, such as a legislator, community leader, or major funder
- Releasing studies and statistics that demonstrate a positive impact on the economy
- Promoting client and graduate milestones, such as first-round funding, second-round funding, patents, or IPOs
- Hosting a training event or open house
- Attending a training event (which establishes your professional credentials)

- Challenge old information?
- Significantly affect people in a positive way?

When you don't have news of your own, look for opportunities to attach a local hook to a national or international story. Regional media outlets generally prefer a local angle to a news event, so they are often eager to hear from community residents who can offer a knowledgeable view of the "big picture." For example, if a governmental organization or a private research group releases a report on entrepreneurship or small business, consider pitching the story to your local media. Provide comments and statistics from your own experiences to support—or sometimes even dispute—the findings of the study.

Defining Your Target Audience

Investors, government officials, local residents, and entrepreneurs are all potential audiences for news about your program. Your communication efforts will be most effective if you determine your target audience before contacting the press, so you can provide the media with the appropriate tools to deliver your message to the people you want to reach.

Want to pique the interest of potential clients? Consider pitching a story showcasing the success of an existing client or graduate. Zero in on one of your outstanding companies and dangle the story before a newspaper or magazine editor.

Trying to gain community support? Gather statistics that highlight your program's economic impact. Present this information in a news release, and send it to local and regional media outlets. This type of news is particularly effective when linked to a broader issue. For example, if unemployment is rising in your area, impressive job creation numbers will make editors—and community leaders—take notice.

Want to reach potential stakeholders or service providers? Volunteer as a speaker for a local organization whose membership includes prominent business leaders. Since the media often cover these events, the resulting coverage can help you build your image as a recognized leader in the field. The more you are able to spread the word about your organization's successes, the more other businesspeople will want to associate with your program and your clients.

Selecting Media Outlets

After you determine your target audience, it's time to develop a plan for reaching it. Sometimes print publications are the obvious route for delivering your news, while other times radio or television might be the most appropriate medium. Begin by compiling a list of all print, radio, and television media in your region. If you need help locating local and regional news outlets, ask a librarian to help you find an appropriate media directory.

Your media list should include contact information for the appropriate person at each outlet—often a business or economic development reporter. You can usually find this information on the news organization's Web site or by calling the media outlet. Identifying the appropriate contact is an important part of developing your media list because it ensures your message will reach the right desk. Don't assume that reporters will forward your news to the correct person.

When compiling your list, don't overlook trade publications and business journals. If one of your clients has launched a new software product for architects, the news might interest both computer magazines and architectural journals. Media directories often include such specialty publications. Be sure to add appropriate online publications to your media list; Web publications can reach millions of readers daily. Also, remember to include local offices of national and international wire services—such as Associated Press, Reuters, Dow Jones, and Bloomberg—when your news is of interest to more than just your local audience.

To jumpstart your list, call the public relations department of a large institution in your area, such as a university, corporation, or hospital, and ask if they will share updated media lists with you. Then, confirm that their contacts are current and relevant to you. Because reporters and editors change assignments often, you should check the accuracy of your media list before you send a mailing or make a phone call. Updating your media list is an excellent task for a student intern.

Contacting the Media

Once you have your contact numbers in hand, it's time to use them. Call editors and reporters to introduce yourself and your program. Invite them to tour the incubator. You might want to give them a press kit, which contains basic information about your incubator that will not change often—a handy reference for journalists working on a tight deadline. (See "What to Put in a Press Kit" on page 74.)

This initial contact, though, is as much for you as it is for the reporter or editor. You can learn more about each reporter's interests and needs, including deadlines and his or her preferred method for receiving news announcements. Also find out about the publication's or station's general scope of coverage; targeting your news to the needs and formats of each outlet will increase your chances of getting coverage.

Some journalists accept faxes. Others prefer e-mail or snail mail. In general, if e-mailing news to a reporter, copy your release into the body of a message. Do not send attachments unless specifically requested. Some reporters cannot download large files, and many delete unsolicited attachments unread. Reporters are more interested in your message than in its presentation. However, if you wish to preserve your formatting, place your news release on your Web site and send reporters the direct link.

You may want to hand deliver your news—not every time, just occasionally—to make a lasting impression. Keep the contact friendly but brief, and don't call or visit during deadlines. Bring along a business card for the reporter's files, so he or she will be able to contact you whenever the need arises.

What to Put in a Press Kit

In a sturdy, attractive folder, arrange:
- Your business card
- Fact sheet with basic information about the incubator: who you are, what you do, where you're located, and how to contact you
- Your brochure
- A list of client companies
- A list of partners and/or sponsors
- A recent press release
- A page of client testimonials
- Reprints of newspaper or magazine articles about the incubator
- Photos of the incubator and/or a professional studio portrait of the incubator director

Distributing the News

But how do you get the news to reporters? Here are some of the most common methods for disseminating news. Each of these tools has a slightly different objective, so styles and formats differ.

News releases. News releases (sometimes called press releases) are one- or two-page briefs that announce upcoming events, report on recent activities or accomplishments, or describe potential news or feature stories. Many editors use releases as a platform on which to build their own articles, while others run well-written announcements as submitted.

News releases typically answer the basic news questions (i.e., who? what? when? where? why? how?) and are often written as news or feature stories. When your goal is to alert the media of an upcoming event, you may wish to submit a more specialized news release that provides them with just the information they need to participate. Two such releases are media advisories—brief, bulleted releases that alert the media of an upcoming event—and media availabilities, releases that introduce an expert who can comment on a current news event or issue.

Most media outlets receive more news releases than they can use. Therefore, reporters are more likely to use self-contained releases that require little editing than those that leave basic questions unanswered or read like advertisements. You may wish to read several examples of short articles in local publications to learn more about the effective organization of a news story. To further your chances of having a well-written news release published, use the Associated Press Stylebook. This standard newsroom reference is available from bookstores.

Some general points to remember about news releases:
- Print your release on your program's

Anatomy of a News Release

Every news release should include:

- **The current date.**
- **Date for release.** Decide when you want the information to be published or aired. If you're announcing an upcoming speaker or award winner, you may want the information "embargoed" until shortly before the event. Embargoed means the information is available to news organizations for planning, but the media may not report on it until the date you specify. However, bear in mind that embargo dates could be overlooked.
- **Contact information.** Include the name, title, phone number, fax number, and e-mail address of the appropriate spokesperson. Be sure this information is accurate and use a contact who is readily available. A reporter on a tight deadline may abandon the story if no one is available quickly.
- **Headline.** Come up with a catchy headline that demonstrates the story's newsworthiness and catches the reader's attention. The headline should be in bold type and underlined.
- **Dateline.** This is your city, in capital letters, and the abbreviation of your state or country in lowercase letters. It immediately precedes the opening paragraph. Refer to The Associated Press Stylebook for rules on inclusion of city, state, and country information.
- **Lede.** This is the first paragraph of a news release. It should summarize your news in a concise, interesting way. A straight news lede provides the basic facts. A feature-type lede asks a question or states a surprising fact that draws in the reader. In this case, the second paragraph contains the straight information.
- **Body.** The body further explains why the news is relevant to readers and provides supporting facts. It usually includes quotes from key people. An effective quote should add interest, not just state the obvious.
- **Closing.** The closing suggests a next step, such as where to get more information, or reiterates the significance of the news.

Sample news releases are included on the CD-ROM at the back of this book.

---

letterhead. Be sure to include your NBIA member logo, since membership in a reputable organization increases your credibility. Refer to the CD-ROM included with this book for information about how to access this logo.

- Always double-space your release. If it runs more than one page, type the word "more" at the bottom of page one and "###" or "30" at the end of the release. Try to limit your releases to two pages.
- Keep in mind that deadlines vary widely among publications and allow sufficient time for an editor to assign the story. A monthly magazine may need a news release months in advance, while a daily newspaper usually requires only about a week's notice. Maintaining ongoing relationships with local media representatives will keep you informed about their production schedules.
- Define your work in simple, everyday terms and keep industry jargon to a minimum. If you must use technical terms, include a glossary.

Refer to the CD-ROM included with this book for examples of news releases, as well as stock text about incubation and NBIA.

News/feature story pitches. You've just acquired an abandoned storefront on Main Street. The building has long been a source of debate, so this is hot, breaking news. Pitch the story directly to the media. By this time, you should have established personal relationships with reporters. Contact one—or maybe even several. Although journalists usually prefer an exclusive story, few will refuse to do a follow-up simply because they did not receive the news first. Introduce the potential story with written material and follow up with a phone call.

Editorial page contributions. Among business and community leaders, the editorial page is one of the most widely read sections of the newspaper. Thus, letters to the editor or opinion-editorial pieces—also known as op-eds—provide great avenues for getting your message out. There are several situations that merit a letter:

- **A simple thank-you.** Has a group or individual significantly helped your program? Did the community respond favorably to an incubator-sponsored workshop? If so, take a moment to write a warm, public thank you.
- **A response.** If you received good news coverage, write a letter thanking the newspaper and include more information, if possible. For example, "Your reporter did an excellent job explaining business

News Release Add-Ons

When issuing a news release, you can further entice editors by sending along graphics, photographs, or other supporting documents. Often, an editor will run a story that has artwork rather than one that does not simply because it will provide more visual interest on the page than a text-only story. Some examples of supporting documents include:

- **Photographs, logos, or other graphic images**. Be sure to provide complete caption and photographer's credit information. The first sentence of the caption should describe the person, event, or activity shown in the photo. All recognizable people should be identified from left to right.
- **Fact sheet.** A one-page document that provides key information about your program and the incubation industry. This fact sheet may contain information about your mission, accomplishments, activities, etc. You also may want to include NBIA's Incubation FAQ (available at www.nbia.org) to offer background on the incubation industry in general.
- **Annual report.** If your program's annual report is straightforward and easy to read, you may include it with your news release in lieu of a fact sheet. Your annual report should contain vital statistics about your program in a format that can be referenced quickly and easily.
- **Graphics** that highlight the data presented in your release.
- **Biographies** of key individuals.
- **Background information** about your incubator, clients, and graduates.

If you are sending material to reporters electronically, do not include supplemental materials in the initial message. Offer to send the files separately. You should also check with the reporter or editor to determine the media outlet's capacity to open your graphics files. Keep in mind that print publications require artwork that is saved at a much higher resolution than artwork that is used on the Web. In general, print publications require images that are at least five inches by seven inches saved as high-resolution JPGs or TIFFs—at least three hundred dots per inch, or dpi. Web graphics usually are displayed at only seventy-two dpi.

incubation in the June 5 article, 'Incubation in Action.' Perhaps your readers would be interested in knowing that we have an affiliate program that serves out-of-house clients."

Conversely, if you are unhappy with a story, write a letter that points out any errors and presents the correct information. Most likely, the mistake was unintentional. You'll have to deal with the reporter again, so keep a professional tone. For example, you might write, "The June 5 article, 'Incubation in Action,' contained an error. We serve 30 in-house clients, not three, as reported."

For glaring inaccuracies, call the editor personally. He or she will usually publish a correction. Also, consider whether the inaccuracy merits a correction or whether it is so minor you can live with it. You may decide to simply call a friendly reporter with thanks for a story and clarification "for future use."

- **A comment.** Speak out in support of small businesses. Perhaps your local chamber of commerce is focusing all its efforts on large companies, and community residents are voicing complaints. Add your voice to the debate in a noncontroversial manner. For example, "In response to Mr. Smith's letter in the June 5 issue of your paper, I think it's important to note that small businesses create numerous jobs and contribute significantly to our tax base." Cite statistics and stress the need for balance in economic development strategies.

Many local, regional, and national media outlets also run opinion-editorial articles. These short pieces—typically six hundred to eight hundred words—are an effective way to share your opinion about key issues with local leaders and the general public. Op-ed articles often are used to provide local angles to hot national issues. Many publications require op-ed pieces to be exclusive to their readership, so be sure to check all requirements before submitting an article to more than one outlet.

Community calendar announcements. Many radio stations and some television stations promote community events through a free community calendar service (also known as public service announcements or PSAs). A PSA is generally a short—one minute or less—television or radio announcement about a public service. There's no cost for a PSA, but the announcement must benefit the community. For example, if you are sponsoring a free or low-cost workshop for start-ups or if your nonprofit program is seeking low-income clients, you have the makings of a community calendar listing.

The availability of this service varies; some stations will carry only arts and entertainment events, while others will promote only events sponsored by nonprofit organizations. Be sure to check the specific guidelines of your local stations before submitting an announcement. As with news releases, the media receive many more PSAs than they can use. You will increase your chances of being included in the community calendar by submitting all the basic information about the event, as well as a contact name and phone number, in the format the station requests.

Generally, stations need community calendar information at least two to four weeks before an event to allow adequate production time. Some media outlets may require up to eight weeks of lead time, so the earlier you get the information to the stations, the more likely they are to use it.

Refer to the CD-ROM included with this book for an example of a PSA issued by an NBIA member.

Radio and Television Promotions

Although all media outlets share a common goal of supplying news to the community, the needs of the broadcast media differ from those of print publications. Because the amount of airtime available for broadcast news programs is limited, stories and announcements written for radio and/or television require fewer words. The following guidelines deal specifically with promoting your incubation program and your clients to radio and television outlets.

In radio, the station's primary format (e.g., news, talk, country, easy listening, top-40) and target demographic will determine the type of news stories it reports. A primarily news-oriented station is more likely to cover business news than a station that is primarily music-oriented. However, if you have a story that could be of general interest (e.g., a new incubator will bring five hundred new jobs to the area), even a non-news station may be interested in reporting it.

The format of TV news coverage varies from station to station. Watch local news programs for a few days to determine how your news fits into your local station's coverage. Are there more local stories than national stories? Human-interest stories (or even whole programs devoted to human-interest material)? Business news? When you determine how your news fits into the station's format, use this information to pitch your idea to the news department. Assignment editors will be more likely to consider using your story if you make it fit their style.

Keep your news releases and pitches short. A good rule of thumb when timing your text is that seventy words equal about one minute of voice-over copy. The less work a station has to do to make your information ready for airing, the more likely it will be to use it. In addition to a standard news release, you should consider sending radio and TV stations an abbreviated version containing only the most essential information.

Weigh the pros and cons of paid commercials and underwriting. Paying for good public relations is never as nice as getting it for free, but it may sometimes be beneficial. If you are trying to get a large turnout for a particular event that may be of interest to a large portion of the general public (e.g., a job fair or business expo at a large venue), you may want to look into advertising options. Generally, radio is a much cheaper way to reach people than television.

Underwriting business- or finance-oriented programs on your local public radio and/or television station is another way to get your name before your community. As an underwriter, your message would air before, during, and/or after specific programs on Public Broadcasting System and National Public Radio affiliates in the United States. Underwriting usually involves a long-term contract (six months to one year), so this type of promotion would be useful for generating familiarity with your incubator over a period of time. Specific PBS shows a business incubator might consider underwriting include *The NewsHour with Jim Lehrer*, *Washington Week*, and *The Nightly Business Report*. NPR programs that might make a good pairing with business incubation include *Morning Edition*, *All Things Considered*, and *Talk of the Nation*. (For an example of such underwriting, see page 45.)

News Conferences

News conferences are planned events that feature speakers and/or showcase a newsworthy happening. Although you don't want to overuse these events, a news conference is a useful way to announce the opening of a new facility, the beginning of construction, or a visit by an important person. Send out brief, friendly invitations to local print, radio, and television journalists at least a week in advance. Your invitations should summarize the reason for the event, state where and when it will be held, and include contact information. If your town has a local Associated Press bureau, ask to have your event included on its Daybook, a daily listing of news events that are scheduled in the community. Many local media outlets use the Daybook when deciding what events to cover.

News conferences work best when there is a visual component to the story, so they are often great tools for generating television coverage. Make it fun—for example, invite a reporter to try out a client's product or service.

Working With the Media

Your patience and willingness to work with reporters will benefit your program and your clients in the long run. Each quote you give has an impact—it establishes you as an expert in your field. If you're responsive to the needs of the media, you'll soon find that reporters begin calling you, unsolicited, for interviews. They will hand you the golden opportunity to laud your program, your clients, and business incubation in general.

Prepare yourself, your staff, and your clients for calls from the media before those calls come. Designate one staff member as spokesperson for the program, and encourage client companies to do the same. It's also a good idea to select one or two client companies that are willing to do media interviews about their experiences with your program. Arm them with the statistics and facts they'll need to support their comments. Having designated spokespeople will help ensure that both you and your clients provide consistent, credible information over time.

To help your clients learn more about media relations, conduct an informal meeting or host a brown bag luncheon. Share some of the tips you've learned here. Give them copies of your annual report. Don't be shy about asking them to mention the incubator during interviews—if you've done your job well, they'll be happy to acknowledge you publicly.

Below are some general tips that can help you improve your relationships with all segments of the media. Remember, though, you will receive your best news coverage if you determine the specific needs of local reporters and follow their preferences precisely.

- Make a genuine effort to help reporters.

Holding a News Conference

- **Determine who will speak at the event.** Limit the number of speakers to three. Make sure each person prepares a statement in advance. At the news conference, introduce each speaker, stating name, title, affiliation, and credentials. Give reporters a list of speakers (including correct spellings, titles, and affiliations).
- **Schedule for optimum coverage.** To get coverage on the evening news or in the morning newspaper, check the deadlines of your target news organization(s) and plan your conference accordingly.
- **Select a convenient location.** Include directions in your invitations. Keep in mind that reporters need electrical outlets for light and audio equipment. TV reporters need ample space to set up cameras.
- **Offer refreshments.** Even something as simple as coffee and doughnuts will increase your turnout. Your invitation should mention that refreshments will be available.
- **Illustrate your point.** Encourage speakers to use photos, charts, or other visual aids. Prepare a press packet that includes a short news release, fact sheet(s), speaker biographies, and copies of the visual aids. If possible, include copies of the speakers' comments.
- **Start on time.** Journalists are busy people on deadlines. Also, keep it short—allow no more than twenty minutes for presentations (total), followed by a ten minute question-and-answer period. If reporters want more information, they'll stay later to conduct interviews.

- Be available and responsive.
- Don't expect coverage every time you issue a news release. Don't call reporters to ask when your news release will run.
- Put a human face on your news. Statistics and policy statements provide necessary background information, but a compelling human-interest story is more likely to catch an editor's eye.
- Never call during deadline unless you have spectacular, late-breaking news to add. An occasional follow-up call to answer questions about news releases or article pitches is permissible at other times, unless the reporter says otherwise.
- Include reporters on your program's general mailing list. Newsletters and other mailings (when appropriate) can teach business reporters more about your program over time.
- Be prepared to educate reporters about business incubation in general as well as about your specific program. If you need more information about the industry as a whole, see the Incubation FAQ on the NBIA Web site at *www.nbia.org*. Refer to the CD-ROM included with this book for stock text about business incubation.

Tips for Media Interviews

Whether you're expecting it or not, you're likely to find yourself on the phone with a reporter sooner or later. If you're prepared for these calls, you'll be able to use the interview as an opportunity to get the word out about your program and your clients. When an interview is scheduled in advance, try to determine the scope of the article and develop a clear objective about what you want to say. Make sure the evidence to support your main points is readily available. You should be responsive to the reporter's questions, but you can often use the key points you want to communicate to explain, clarify, or amplify your answers.

Sometimes, reporters ask difficult questions. Anticipate the tough questions and prepare your answers. If possible, practice your answers before the interview. If you don't know the answer to a question, say so. Get back to the reporter as quickly as possible with the information. If you cannot comment on an issue, tell the reporter why (e.g., it is a confidential personnel matter, the problem is still being examined, etc.). Do not say, "No comment." It makes you sound like you're hiding something. If you can release more information later, do so.

Stop speaking once you have answered a question. Don't ramble to fill the silence. If you do not want your words printed or broadcasted, do not say them. Do not rely on "off-the-record" discussions. (Off-the-record comments are not supposed to be reported to the public, but human error is always a possibility.) Keep your answers short and to the point. Make yourself quotable. Do not leave it up to reporters to pull out what is most important to quote.

If you receive an unexpected call from the media, do not feel pressured to answer tough questions without time to prepare. If you are not prepared, schedule another time for the interview. Remember, reporters are often on tight deadlines, so gather your thoughts and get back in touch with them quickly.

How to Handle Bad News

Mistakes happen, companies fail, crises occur. Life is not always good—and neither is the news. However, bad news and good news usually balance out over time. If you handle the media well during times of crisis, local reporters and the community will be more likely to follow your successes as well. Following are some general tips for dealing with the media in times of crisis.

- **Take the initiative** in delivering the news—whether good or bad. If you report bad news, you can make sure you have the opportunity to tell your side of the story.
- **Don't lie or be evasive**, or you'll lose credibility. If your organization comes under fire, be up front and honest. Add a positive spin. For example, when the dot-com bust resulted in negative media coverage about the incubation industry, NBIA readily acknowledged that not all incubators succeed. However, the association also provided statistics that clearly demonstrated the positive economic value of incubation in general.
- **Find a solution.** Some problems can be fixed—or at least minimized—with creative thinking on your part. If the media catches wind of such a problem, let them know how the issue is being addressed. Your willingness to take action is a sign of effective leadership.
- **Don't talk under pressure.** When you are under fire and a reporter calls, delay the interview, if possible. Make an appointment, gather your thoughts, hone your message, and then do the interview. Don't avoid the interview altogether—this suggests you have something to hide. Keep the reporter's deadline in mind and be as flexible as possible.

APPENDIX B
Sources

These books, magazines, and Web sites were either quoted in the text or provided helpful background information in the course of researching and writing this book.

Beckwith, Harry. *Selling the Invisible: A Field Guide to Modern Marketing*. New York: Warner Books, 1997.

Creative Research Services. "Survey Design." www.surveysystem.com/sdesign.htm.

Gerl, Ellen. "20 Questions: Developing Your Marketing Focus." *NBIA Review* 12:1 (January/February 1996).

Hayhow, Sally. "Fishing for Future Clients." *NBIA Review* 14:5 (October 1998).

Kiernan, Nancy Ellen. Tipsheet #53, "Designing a Survey to Increase Response and Reliability." University Park: Penn State Cooperative Extension, 2001. www.extension.psu.edu/evaluation/pdf/TS53.pdf.

Konrath, Jill. "How to Write a Strong Value Proposition." www.sideroad.com/Sales/value_proposition.html.

Kotler, Philip. *Marketing for Nonprofit Organizations*. Englewood Cliffs, NJ: Prentice-Hall, 1975.

—. *Ten Deadly Marketing Sins: Signs and Solutions*. Hoboken, NJ: John Wiley & Sons, 2004.

—, and Paul N. Bloom. *Marketing Professional Services*. Englewood Cliffs, NJ: Prentice-Hall, 1984.

—, and Sidney J. Levy. "Broadening the Concept of Marketing." In *Marketing in Nonprofit Organizations*, ed. Patrick J. Montana, 3–15. New York: AMACOM, 1978.

Lake, Laura. "Market Segmentation for the Small Business." marketing.about.com/cs/sbmarketing/a/smbizmrktseg.htm.

Leones, Julie. "A Guide to Designing and Conducting Visitor Surveys." Tucson: Arizona Cooperative Extension, College of Agriculture, The University of Arizona, 1998. ag.arizona.edu/pubs/marketing/az1056/.

Levinson, Jay Conrad. *Guerrilla Marketing, Completely Revised and Updated Third Edition*. New York: Houghton Mifflin, 1998.

Marcure, Judy. *Marketing Scientific Results & Services: A Toolkit, 2nd Edition*. Sydney, Australia: Calibre Communications, 2004.

McKenna, Regis. *Relationship Marketing: Successful Strategies for the Age of the Customer*. Reading, MA: Addison-Wesley Publishing Company, 1991.

Mohr, Jakki J., Sanjit Sengupta, and Stanley Slater. *Marketing of High Technology Products and Innovations, 2nd ed*. Upper Saddle River, NJ: Pearson Prentice Hall, 2001, 2005.

National Business Incubation Association. "Snap Your Way Onto the Front Page." *NBIA Review*: 17:6 (December 2001).

Shapiro, Benson P. "Marketing for Nonprofit Organizations." In *Marketing in Nonprofit Organizations*, ed. Patrick J. Montana, 16–30. New York: AMACOM, 1978.

The Survey System. "Survey Design." From The Survey System's Tutorial, revised June 2005. www.surveysystem.com/sdesign.htm/.

Tiffany, Laura, compiler. "How to Create a Marketing Plan." Entrepreneur.com: August 7, 2001. www.entrepreneur.com/article/0,4621,291706,00.html.

Wikipedia. "Market segment." en.wikipedia.org/wiki/Market_segment.

— "Marketing mix." en.wikipedia.org/wiki/Marketing_mix.

— "Relationship marketing." en.wikipedia.org/wiki/Relationship_marketing.

Index

Page numbers in parentheses indicate that the subject is part of a sidebar.

A

@Wales Digital Media Initiative, v, vii, viii, 2, 18, 35, 39, 49, 50

Adirondack Regional Business Incubator, ix, 52-54

Advanced Technology Development Center, vii, (16), 29, (31), (46), 47-48, 58-59, 60

advertising, 32, 43, 43-48, (48), (49), 54, 56, 59, 63-64, 78

advisory board, incubator, 34, 61, 62, (63)

affiliate programs, 43, 77

Allen, Charles, vii, (44)

Amoskeag Business Incubator, viii, 2, 8, 18, 23, 34, 35, 41, 47, 56

anchor tenants, 66

angel investors, (5), 8, (37), 49, (50), 66-67

ANGLE Technology, ix, 4, 16, 27, (31), 33, (36)

annual reports, (50), 58, 64-65, (65), (76), 79

Antoniades, Tony, vii, (16), 29, (31), (46), 47-48, 58-59, 60

Applied Process Engineering Laboratory, vii, ix, (44)

associations, as research sources, (5), 7-8, 18

Athens Area Chamber of Commerce, ix

Augustine, John L., III, vii, 65

awards, 52, 58, 64, (75)

B

banners, 47, (50)

Barral, Judith, vii, 41

Barz, Wayne, vii, 68

Barzilai-Abileah, Hilla, vii, 62-63

Ben Franklin Technology Partners of Northeast Pennsylvania, vii, 68

Birkill, Anne-Marie, vii

board of directors, 2, 28, 29, (31), 41, (63), 66, 69

branding, 39-42, (40), 47, 68

Breedlove, Patti, vii, (20), 23-24

brochures, (13), (16), 21, 32, 33, (33), 34, 41, (50), 54, (57), 58-60, (63), 64, (65), (74)

budget, marketing, 4, (15), 33-34, 45, 54, 55, (57), 64

Business Cluster Development, vii, 3

business plan, incubator, 27

Business Technology Center of Los Angeles County, viii, 34, (42), 56, 66

Business Technology Center, The, vii, (36-37)

Business, Industry & Entrepreneurship Center, ix, 6, (6)

C

calendar, marketing, 32-33

Canterbury Enterprise Hub, 30, 32, 62, 66

Cattey, David J., vii

CD-ROMs, as marketing tools, 43, 59

Central Valley Business Incubator, viii, (40), 46, 51

Ceramics Corridor Innovation Centers, ix, 44

chambers of commerce, (5), 7, 32, 48, 60, 61

Clark, Linda J., vii, (28), 29, 32-33, 46

Clark, Steven, vii, (37)

client services, general, 4, 5, 8, 9, 10-11, 12, 14, 16-17, 22, (22), 23-24, 28, 29, (30), (36-37), 62

clients, identifying, 2, 4, 5, 8, 13, 15-18, 29-30, (30), 53-54, 55-56, 60, 61, 63

Cochrane, Sandra, vii

collateral, marketing, (15), (16), 41, 55, 58-59, (63), (76)

Community Development Commission of Los Angeles County, viii, 34, 56
competitions as promotions, (10), 21, (50), 52
competitors, 1, 16, 19, (20), (30), 31, 56
consultant, marketing, 7, 8, 11, 12, 14, (15), (22), (28), 34
Contacts Count, ix, 66, (67)
cooperative marketing, (33), (37), 42, 45-46, (46), 47-48, 54-56, 56-58, 61, 62, 62-64, 64-65, (65), 66-68
Cooperhouse, Lou, vii, 9, 12, 14, 17, 24, (44)
Cowley College, ix, 6, (6)

D

D'Agostino, Charles F., vii, 1, 24, (33), 35, 42, (44), 51, 55, 56, 58, 65, 68
data, marketing, 3, 4, 5, (5), 6, (6), 7, (7), 8, 11, 12, 13, 14, (22), 35, 49, 64, (76)
database, marketing, 18, (25), 35, 60, 62-63
DeDiemar, Jeanette, vii
design, *See* graphic design
DeYoung, Jan, vii, 56-57
direct mail, 14, (48), 48-49, (50)
Doell, Glenn, vii, 58
Drachnik, Scott J., vii, 6
Dykes, Carol Ann, vii

E

Economic Development Center of St. Charles County, vii, 6
editorial page contributions, (50), 76
educational programs, *See* outreach; seminars and training programs
e-mail marketing, 1, 13, 34, (48), 49, (50), 60
e-mail services, (25), 49, 60
e-newsletters, (25), 34, 43, 60
entrepreneurial pool, *See* clients, identifying
evaluation, incubator performance, 3, 11, 21, 27
events, (15), 18, 24, 33, 34, 43, 49-50, (50), 51-53, (53), 66

F

facility, incubator, 10, 17, 23, (36), 39, (63)
Fairfax Innovation Center, vii, 41
feasibility study, 4, 16, 52
fee structuring, *See* pricing
firms, marketing/public relations, 11, 12, 13, (15), (20), 20, (25), 33, 34, 41, 43
Fitzsimons Redevelopment Authority, viii, 54
Flemal, Agnes, vii
Florida/NASA Business Incubation Center, ix
focus groups, 9, 11, 12, 13, 14, 17, 18
Four Ps, 32
Frison, Paul M., vii, 63, 64
funding sources/fundraising, incubator, (22), 43, 44, 51, 52, 54, 62
Furtado, Kelli, viii, 46, 51

G

giveaways, (33), 47-48, (50)
goals, marketing, 27, (28), 29, 32, 35, 40, (55)
goals, research, 8, 8-11
Graham, Colin, viii
graphic design, 21, 41, 53, 59, (59), 60, 61, (61), 62, 64
graphic identity, (13), 41, 61
Greater Reston Chamber of Commerce, ix, 41
Greene, Tweed & Co., vii, 58
Greenwood Consulting Group, viii, 5
Greenwood, Jim, viii, 5
Gulf Coast Business Technology Center, viii
Gustafson, Julie, viii, 2, 8, 17, 23, 34, 35, 42, 47, 56, 60
Gwinnett Innovation Park, viii, 3, (13), 21, 40, (40)

H

Haynes, Tim, viii, (37)
Herron, Bonnie, viii, 3-4, (13), 20-21, 40, (40)
Hess, Vic, viii, 17
High Tech Rochester, ix, (53)

Hisrich, Robert, viii, 4, 7, (36-37), 39, 40, 42, (42), 43, 44, 45, 47, 48-49, 65
Hobbs, Ed, viii, 46-47, 64
Houston Technology Center, vii, 62-64
Howard County Economic Development Agency, viii, 17

I

i.lab Incubator, viii, (40)
INC.*spire*, ix, 41
incubation associations, 8, 10, 12, 14, (20), 21, 75
incubator analysis, 30-32, (31), (36-37)
incubator description, 29, (31)
incubator development, general, 4, 10, 11, 12, 65
incubator without walls, 9, 51
Indiana University Emerging Technologies Center, viii, 11, 14, (15), (25), 41
Innovation Center @ Wilkes-Barre, vii, 65
Innovation Centre Sunshine Coast, viii
interviews, market research, 8, 12, 14, (15), 21, 23, 24
interviews, media, 79, 80, 81
Ison, Lisa, viii, 43-44, 47

J

Jenings, Vicki, viii, 54, 55
Jones, Evan M., viii, 2, 18, 35, 39, 50

K

King, Deborah L., viii, 51, 60-61
kitchen incubator, 9, (40), 56-57

L

LaPan, Karl R., viii, 45
Lauffer, Carol Kraus, vii, 3, 5
Lennox Tech Enterprise Center, ix, (53)
letters to the editor, 76-77
Lieberman, Mark, viii, 34, (42), 56, 66-67
logos, (15), 21, 33, 41, 42, 45, (46), 47, (63), 64, 68, 75
Lohr, David R., viii

Long, Mark S., viii, 11, 12, 14, (15), (25), 41
Longserre, Marie, viii
Louisiana Business & Technology Center, vii, 1, 24, (33), 35, 42, (44), 55
Louisiana State University, 1, 42, 56
Louisiana Technology Park, viii, (15)
Loy, Stephen, viii, (15)
Lyons, Adele, viii

M

magazine coverage, 57, 72, 73, (74), 75
market description, 29-30
market segmentation, 16-17
marketing collateral, *See* collateral
marketing mix, 32
marketing plan, 27-37
measuring effectiveness of marketing efforts, 35
media outlets, 5, (6), 7, 35, 73
media relations, 56-58, (57), 71-81
MidMichigan Innovation Center, ix, (15), 21-23
Miller, Stuart, ix, 41
Miscenich, Aaron, ix, 54, 55
mistakes, marketing, (42)
Mitchell, Suzanne, ix

N

National Business Incubation Association, 3, 8, 10, 12, 14, (20), 21, 27, 29, 32, (40), 43, 52, (53), (55), 56, 58, 64, 69, 71, 75, (76), 81
name, incubator, (13), 19-21, (40), 40-41
Nashville Business Incubation Center, ix, (10), (25), 32, 52
NBIA, *See* National Business Incubation Association
networking, 2, 3, (15), 18, 24, 49-50, 66
New Century Venture Center, The, viii, 43, 47
New Orleans BioInnovation Center, ix, 54
news conference, (50), 78-79, (79)
news release, 34, 35, (50), 56, (57), 58, (63), 73, (74), 74-75, (75), (76), 78, (79), 80

news, definition of, 71, (72); distribution of, (74), 74-77, (76)
newsletters, (25), 34, 43, (50), 54, (57), 58, 60-62, (61), (63), 64, 80
newspaper coverage, 35, (37), 56-57, 72, (74), 75, 76, (79)
nonresident clients, *See* affiliate programs
Northeast Indiana Innovation Center, viii, 45
Northern Alberta Business Incubator, ix, 29-30, 58

O

O'Neal, Tom, ix
O'Regan, Bonnie, ix
objectives, market research, *See* goals
occupancy rates, (19), 65
Ohio University Innovation Center, vii, (28), 29, 32, 45
opinion-editorial pieces, 76-77, (50)
outreach, (28), 49, 49-50, (53), (55)

P

partners, 2, 8, (16), 18, (25), (30), 34, (36-37), 40, 42, 43, 48, 49, 55, 58, 60, (63), (67), 69, (74)
photography, 34, 56, (57), 59, 60-61, (63), 64, (74), (76), (79)
placement, 32
positioning, 19-23, (20), (22)
press kits, 59, 73, (74)
press release, *See* news release
pricing, 11, 14, (22), (32), (36)
primary research, 4, 8-14, (9), (13)
product, 32, 40, 41
promotion, (19), (25), 32, 43, 45, 51, 77-78; *See also* advertising; competitions; events; giveaways; media relations; newsletters; news release; photography; publicity; seminars and training programs
promotional items, *See* giveaways
public broadcasting, sponsorship, 45-46, 78

public relations, (15), (22), (25), 33, 41, 42, (50), 56-58, (57), 67, 70, 73, 78
public speaking, 2, 34, 46, 55, 65, 80
publications, (50), 58-65, (59), (61), (63), (65); *See also* brochures; e-newsletters; newsletters; reports; Web sites
publicity, 5, 51, 52, 56-58, (57), 71-81

R

radio advertising, *See* advertising
referrals, *See* testimonials; word of mouth
Rensselaer Incubator Program, 58
reports, 64-65, (65), (76), 79
reputation, 1, (20), 29, 39, 42, 56, 58, 67-68, 73
research park, 11, 12, (15)
research sources, 4-8, (5), (6), (7), (13), 24
research, incubation, 8, 10, 11
Roberts, Lisa S., ix, 6, (6), 7
Rubenstein, Lesley Anne, ix, 31-32, 49, 62, 66
rural incubators, 6, 16, (25), 51, 53
Rutgers Food Innovation Center, vii, 9, 17, (44)

S

sampling, 8, 11-12, 13
San Juan College Enterprise Center, ix, 8, (15), (22), 27, 34
Santa Fe Business Incubator, viii
Schutt, Donald C., ix, (15), 21
Schwanbeck, Dar, ix, 29-30, 58-59, 60
secondary research, 4, 5, 5-8, (7)
self-sustainability, (22), 24-25
seminars and training programs, 49, 49-51, (50), (53), 55, 52
service providers, 8, 29, 30, (30), (33), (36), 39, 55, 56, 60, 66, 73
Sid Martin Biotechnology Incubator, vii, (15), (20), 23
signage, 43, 46-47, (50)
Simon, Jennifer, ix
Small Business Development Centers, 6, 35

Smith, Lisa S., ix, 4, 6, 7, 10, 11, 12, 16, 17, 18, 27, 28, (31), 32, 33, 35, (36)
Southwest Michigan Innovation Center, vii
special-focus incubator, 2, 8, 17, (40)
sponsors, 7, 18, 20, (30), 31, 33, (36-37), 39, (40), 41, 42, 44, (46), 48, 51, (53), 56, 59, 60, 62, (63), 66, (74)
Springfield Business Incubator, viii, 51, 60
Springfield Technical Community College, viii, 51, 61
St. Louis Enterprise Centers, vii, 56
stakeholders, 3, 4, 8, 11, (15), 19, 21, (30), (31), 34, (36-37), 60, 64, 73
Stein, Charles, ix, 4, (7), (15), 16-17, 18, (22), (25)
Strategic Development Services, ix, 4, (7), (15), (22), (25)
strategic plan, 27, (28)
strategies, marketing, 27, 29, (31), 32, 33-34, 39-68
student interns, 2, 14, (15), 56, 60, 70, 73
surveys, 4, 5, 8, (9), 11, 12, 13-14, (15), 18, 20, 21, (22), 23, 35
swag, *See* giveaways
SWOT analysis, 30-31, (31)

T

taglines, 41-42, 43, 46, 64
target audience, 72-73
target market, 11, 12, 14, 16, (30), (36-37), 42, (50)
techcenter@UMBC Incubator and Accelerator, ix, 3, 11, 12, 18
TechColumbus, vii, viii, (36-37)
television advertising, *See* advertising
testimonials, (44), (50), (74)
Thames Innovation Centre, ix, 31, 49, 62
Thomas, Tammi L., ix, 3, 11, 12, 14, 18
Thunderbird Global Incubator, viii, 4, (36), 39, (42), 47, 48, 49
Thunderbird School of Global Management, viii, 4, (36), 39, (42)

Toronto Business Development Centre, viii, (40), 46, 64, (65)
tracking marketing results, (25), 34-35, 43, 47, 49, 53-54, 56, 58, 64
trade shows, 33, (33), 42, 47, (50), 54-56, (55)
training programs, *See* seminars and training programs
T-shirts, (46), 47-48

U

University of Central Florida Technology Incubator, vii, ix
University of Florida, vii, (20), 23-24
University of Wisconsin Oshkosh, vii

V

value proposition, (22), (36-37), 45
Virginia Biosciences Development Center, viii
virtual incubator, *See* incubator without walls

W

Wallonia Space Logistics, vii
Walters, Mildred, ix, (10), (25), 32, 52
Watkins, Megan, ix, 49
Waymon, Lynne, ix, 65, (67)
Web sites, incubator, 12, (15), 21, 32, 33, 34, 35, (36-37), 41, 42, (44), 49, (50), (57), 59, 60, 62-64, (63), 74
Welch, Jasper, ix, 8, 11, (15), (22), 27-28, 34
Wetenhall, Paul, ix, (53)
Wilder, Jon M., ix, 44
Wohl, Peter, ix, 52-54
Women's Technology Cluster, ix, 49
word of mouth, 18, 19, (19), 35, 39, (44), (53), 57, 60, 65, 68; *See also* testimonials
workshops, *See* seminars and training programs
writing, resources, 59

Z

Zilar, Mary, ix

Other Books Published by the National Business Incubation Association

Developing a Business Incubation Program: Insights and Advice for Communities

2005 Compensation Survey of Incubation Executives

The Incubation Edge: How Incubator Quality and Regional Capacity Affect Technology Company Performance

A Comprehensive Guide to Business Incubation, Completely Revised 2nd Edition

Incubation in Evolution: Strategies and Lessons Learned in Four Countries

Self-Evaluation Workbook for Business Incubators

Incubating Technology Businesses: A National Benchmarking Study

2002 State of the Business Incubation Industry

A Brief History of Business Incubation in the United States

Does Technology Incubation Work? A Critical Review of the Evidence

Put It in Writing: Crafting Policies, Agreements, and Contracts for Your Incubator

Incorporating Your Business Incubation Program: How Tax Status and Business Entity Affect Operations

Technology Commercialization Through New Company Formation: Why U.S. Universities Are Incubating Companies

Incubating in Rural Areas: Challenges and Keys to Success

Best Practices in Action: Guidelines for Implementing First-Class Business Incubation Programs

Incubating the Arts: Establishing a Program to Help Artists and Arts Organizations Become Viable Businesses

Bricks & Mortar: Renovating or Building a Business Incubation Facility

Human Resources: Finding the Right Staff for Your Incubator

Business Incubation Works

The Art & Craft of Technology Business Incubation: Best Practices, Strategies, and Tools from More Than 50 Programs

Find these titles and others at www.nbia.org.